THE MILITARY STRATEGY OF THE *ARTHAŚĀSTRA*

THE MILITARY STRATEGY OF THE *ARTHAŚĀSTRA*

Col Harjeet Singh

PENTAGON PRESS

THE MILITARY STRATEGY OF THE ARTHAŚĀSTRA
by Col Harjeet Singh

ISBN 978-81-8274-698-5

First Edition 2012

Published by

PENTAGON PRESS
206, Peacock Lane, Shahpur Jat
New Delhi-110 049
Tel.: 011-6470 6243, 2649 1568
Telefax: 011-2649 0600
e-mail: rajan@pentagon-press.com

Printed at Aegean Offset Printers, Greater Noida, U.P.

PREFACE

Since its first publication in English, in 1915 after its discovery in 1904, the *Arthaśāstra* has been the object of critical study. The singular credit for the uncovering of the ancient text and its translation goes to Dr. Rudrapatnam Shamashastry of Mysore who not only discovered the manuscript but, through its publication, heralded a new perspective on Indian administration and statecraft. Subsequently, there have been other works and critical commentaries on the contents of the *Arthaśāstra*. The problem of translating the original manuscripts, which were in Sanskrit and the dialectic style adopted by Chānakya/Kautilya (its author), made the accurate rendering of its contents an arduous proposition. The *Arthaśāstra* is a difficult text and, in many instances, it is challenging to discern the exact meaning of the author. This led to various interpretations of the book. Nevertheless, this work initiated a strategic intellectual tradition for India. (The names Chānakya and Kautilya are used interchangeably in this book).

The *Arthaśāstra* is daunting in its scope and range of subject matter. It includes a good deal of prescriptive tabular material on such non-military topics as civil punishments, tax rates, and even seed preparation for crop planting. It is not merely about political science; it is an economic treatise as well. The book elaborates various economic occupations—agriculture, crafts, mining, trade—and their regulation and taxation. Various infrastructure measures —road and bridge building, water management, agricultural ameliorations—are outlined. State-controlled brothels, bars serving alcoholic beverages and gambling houses are presented as an important source of state revenue. In addition, it contains a large and detailed section on criminal and civil law.

A subsequent work by R.P.Kangle—The Kautilya *Arthaśāstra*—was published in three parts by the University of Bombay, in 1963. The first part encompassed the Sanskrit text, the second part contained the English translation with critical and explanatory notes; and the third part was an analysis of the *Arthaśāstra* dealing with its origin, sources and style while also presenting a broad outline of its content. It has been the generally accepted text, though different scholars have translated the word "*Arthaśāstra*" in different ways. Another useful commentary is by Roger Boesche—'*Arthaśāstra* on War and Diplomacy in Ancient India'. In addition, University of Dhaka-based Rashed Uz Zaman's work, "Kautilya: The Indian Strategic Thinker and Indian Strategic Culture" is one which affirms the extant Kautilyan way of thinking.

Understanding the intent of the *Arthaśāstra* largely depends on grasping the context of the actions on which the writing was based. Kautilya faced an unstructured, dynamic set of conditions at the death of Mahapadma Nanda in about 362 B.C. The just-formed Nanda Empire that stretched across the north of India had fallen into instability, occasioning a rapid succession of rulers and tetrarchs. After Alexander the Great died his empire fragmented into Greek-Persian satrapies, which controlled territories as far as the Indus River. The remainder of the subcontinent was a patchwork of small feuding states and ungoverned lands.

In this state of disruption and decay, Kautilya singly envisioned a great, united nation. His initial attempt to implement this vision through the last of the Nanda kings, Dhanananda, however, was embarrassingly rebuffed. Incensed and vengeful, Kautilya vowed to destroy the Nanda Empire, using Chandragupta Maurya, an ambitious young prince from the western border region, as his primary weapon. In 305 B.C., Seleucus Nicator surrendered much occupied territory as far as the Indus River to Chandragupta, who then turned his attentions eastward, conquering the corroding Nanda Empire.

The *Arthaśāstra*, then, is a compilation of Kautilya's memoirs on how he accomplished this epic feat as well as advice to

Chandragupta on how to consolidate and maintain his power. Kautilya accepted as a starting point that insecurity and instability are the dominant characteristics of the Indian environment. His exposition is the embodiment of ruthless realism, based on bold, pitiless action. Its reliance on duplicity was not artful subterfuge, but deliberate deception and bloody assassination. The ultimate aim remained conquest, pure and simple.

Western scholars had always argued that ancient India had learnt the art of administration from the Greeks ever since they came into contact with them after the invasion of Alexander. But the *Arthaśāstra* shows how even the British had adopted some of the features contained in the treatise for their administration. The *Arthaśāstra*, though primarily concerned with statecraft, has warfare seldom out of its purview. It contains the most complete ideas of government, law and war.

The *Arthaśāstra* is Kautilya's comprehensive record of actions and advice on governing a vast empire, to include military strategy. Its largest sections cover diplomacy and warfare. He advocated prudence in pursuing the two basic foreign policy aims: securing the state's security against foreign aggression; and expanding the state at the expense of other states. To these ends, diplomacy and covert operations (intelligence) are preferable to waging war. Employing guile in statecraft is better than fixating on military force. The ruler and his advisers must carefully calculate the correlation of forces before launching war. Short-term gains through immediate action must be balanced against long-term gains by waiting for the right moment to act.

Almost all nations locate their contemporary political goals within a wider historical framework. Strategists attempt to create a past-present continuum, which enables them to present current political issues in historical terms. The situation in the Indian subcontinent transposes the historical events two millennia past onto the conditions of the present.

Principles of war generally come from the universal purposes of strategy. Strategic thinking is, by its nature, cross-cultural and universal in its intent. Does India have a military tradition that, in part at least, reflects the thinking of Chānakya? The answer is both 'yes' and 'no'. The rationale for both viewpoints will be explained in the ensuing text. Every nation acts to maximize power and self-interest, and therefore moral principles or obligations have little or no force in actions among nations. An understanding of the text of the *Arthaśāstra* reflects an approach to solve problems. With the fundamental aim of national strategy established as conquest, Kautilya determined that all elements of power be directed to that end. In Kautilya's mind, the *vijigisu* (king in search of conquests) faced a challenging world of anarchy, fierce self-interest on the part of absolutely everyone, and deadly, immediate risk at home and abroad. Thus, for the *vijigisu* to survive, much less succeed, he must use every means at his disposal to gain and cement power. In such a context, a ruler must promote the welfare of the people, as the people are the source of his wealth, and wealth makes it possible to finance more conquests. Conquest, in turn, enlarges his domains and brings more subjects under his control, and the cycle can be repeated until there is nothing left to conquer. Only then can real peace be obtained.

Statecraft was a key factor in conquest. Kautilya framed the *vijigisu's* problem as a *mandala*, a finely patterned ring of concentric circles. The *vijigisu* himself was at the centre. Next to him was likely to be an enemy plotting his destruction. Next to that enemy was that enemy's enemy, and the enemy of one's enemy is a friend. Of course, once the extant enemy was disposed off, the problem was reframed because the former ally became a probable enemy. In this ever-threatening situation, peace was preferable to war only insofar as it bought time to recover from a weak position. It was a temporary expedient, and conquest should resume as soon as it is practical, whether by open warfare, pre-emptive surprise strikes, or secret sabotage. Such an aggressive foreign policy was always justified. After all, Kautilya stated that, "Any king whose kingdom shares a common border with the conqueror is an antagonist." This assumption is Clausewitzian strategy turned on its head—instead of all warfare being an instrument of policy; all policy is a means to prosecute war.

Nothing, then, was beneath a potentate's attention. Internal administration of the kingdom was as important as foreign relations, since the resources to conduct conquest must first be controlled and developed. Hence, the *Arthaśāstra* covers diverse subjects and dictates how society functioned, income from crown property, types and purposes of marriages, how to plan a campaign, and how to treat a subjugated population. The *Arthaśāstra* is one of the earliest and most complete treatments of holistic strategic-level leadership in existence. It is also one of the most single-minded works of its kind. Every resource, every element of national power, every waking moment of a ruler's days, should be spent a singular intent: hegemonic conquest. The question arises: Does the *Arthaśāstra* represent current 21st-century thinking of leaders? Some analysts believe that Kautilya's counsel resonates even today with Indian national leaders, as it did for Chandragupta. They hold that the common understanding of Indian culture as non-violent and peace loving is a Western myth. But the genius of Hinduism, the very reason it has survived so long, is that it does not stand up and fight till pushed. It changes and adapts and modernizes and absorbs.

In Kautilyan terms, a nation needs to skilfully employ its strengths against an enemy weakness. The asymmetric approach to conquest was something that Kautilya would have both understood and approved of and fits into contemporary pragmatic Indian culture. In this context, the Indian policy of non-alignment was directly Kautilyan—a means of enhancing security by a low-risk strategy of playing one superpower off against another until India could gain sufficient strength to protect its own security. India's current negotiating strategies on nuclear deterrence, weapons procurement, and international trade issues reflect both Kautilyan trends and India's 21st-century self-perception of its role as an emerging world power. While the *Arthaśāstra* does not offer a full explanation of contemporary Indian culture, it sets forth traditions and background that offer insights into Indian strategic policies and actions even today.

The text of this book is devoid of footnotes since I felt that a continual reference to Books, Chapters and Paragraphs of the original text of the Arthasastra would detract the reader from the issues being discussed.

Kautilya's *Arthaśāstra* can be considered as one of the greatest books of the ancient world encompassing politics, economy, diplomacy and war. The first time that I heard of the *Arthaśāstra* was in 1980, when I was doing the course at the Defence Services Staff College, Wellington. A colleague gave a lecture on the book and left me captivated with the subject as well as despondent that its contents have not received a wider audience in military circles. I am grateful to Rajan Arya of Pentagon Press who exhorted me to undertake this project. My daughter Simran and her husband Priyanshu, who are living in Australia, and my son Gurjeet, who lives in Canada, encouraged me to spend hours reading various books on the subject. Finally, my wife Satwinder ensured that I had no diversions and could single-mindedly spend time on the computer to complete the manuscript. I am grateful to them for propelling me to write this book.

Chandigarh **Colonel Harjeet Singh**
September 2012

CONTENTS

INTRODUCTION

There were at least fourteen other *Arthaśāstra's* prior to the one written by Chanakya. The very first verse of Kautilya's *Arthaśāstra* says:

> "This single treatise (Kautilya's *Arthaśāstra*) on the science of politics has been prepared mostly by bringing together the teachings of as many treatises on the science of politics as have been composed by ancient teachers for the acquisition and protection of the earth"

Kautilya's *Arthaśāstra* is a 'science of politics'—it is a canonical text to help a king in 'the acquisition and protection of the earth'. It could be regarded as the *śāstra* (knowledge) concerned with general well-being on earth and, since state activity alone can make such a well being possible, the protection of the Earth and its acquisition, are declared to be the province of this *śāstra*. In other words, it incorporates timeless laws of politics, economy, diplomacy and war.

The wide range of state activity covered in the *Arthaśāstra* has a two-fold aim. First, it gives out how a ruler should protect his territory, which refers to administration of the state. Second, it avers how territory should be acquired which implies its conquest. This involves a consideration of the foreign policy of the state. The name *Arthaśāstra* for the science of politics and administration finds mention in the epic of Mahabharata. It is, therefore, possible that the precepts of the science of administration and politics may have been framed by the early *purohitas* for the guidance of the kings whom they served.

It is often stated that India lacks a strategic culture. It is like someone claiming to be apolitical, which itself is a political choice. Others see in India a strategic culture that is more distinct and coherent than most nation states. What is strategic culture and how can people draw such diametrically opposite conclusions about India's strategic culture? In order to analyse this dichotomy we need to define what is meant by strategic culture. A commonly understood definition is that it is a set of shared beliefs, assumptions and modes of behaviour, derived from common experience and accepted narratives (both oral and written) that shape collective identity and relationships to other groups, and which determine appropriate ends and means for achieving security objectives. The extent to which it is practiced is another matter.

By this definition India has a strategic culture wherein war and peace are continuing themes. It is an indigenous construct over the millennia, modified considerably by the experience of two centuries of Mughal rule and later by the colonial experience till the middle of the 20th-century. While not celebrating war the culture treats it as acceptable when good fights evil. Indian strategic culture has been comfortable with this contradiction. Both major Indian epics, the Ramayana and the Mahabharata deal with wars and treat rivalries as natural and normal. However, it is the *Arthaśāstra* which forms the foundation of what is intrinsically Indian strategic thought. The *Arthaśāstra* is basically a handbook on efficient statecraft for kings and high-level ministers. It lays the basis for the utilitarian function of the state, preservation of the status quo and affords political legitimacy to state actions.

The manuscript discovered in 1902 by Rudrapatnam Shamasastry advocates a top-down style of governance with little or no representation held by the general populace, and the continual maintenance of a state through energetic leadership and an extensive secret service. Though the king and upper echelons of society involuntarily accepted such authority because of religious ideals, just as much as the general populace did, the *Arthaśāstra* suggests the existence of a small elite with a secular and realist outlook that actively worked to uphold this power scheme and determine the overall course of the kingdom.

The conduct of public life was not to be guided by these rules for individual morality. Management of the state necessitated realism, not idealism. It required prudence and precise calculation of measures undertaken alongside their short and long-term consequences, which formulated the theoretical beginnings of economics. Public welfare was contingent upon the strength of the state. The latter was achieved by internal development or territorial expansion, both of which were realised through power.

The *Arthaśāstra regards* foreign policy as a zero-sum game and the aim of creating a well-run state is to provide the base for expansion. Kautilya deals with all the theoretical possibilities of conducting an expansionist foreign policy. Hence, the prime motive of the state was the never-ending pursuit of *artha*. It is only after dedicating its energies to this end could the state or king then move on to fulfilling *dharma* and *kama*. As such, the *Arthaśāstra* provides extensive coverage on the overall economy, which includes: infrastructure (roadwork, irrigation, forestry, and fortification), weights and measurements, labour and employment, commerce and trade, commodities and agriculture, land use and property laws, money and coinage, interest rates and loan markets, tariffs and taxes, and government expenditures and the treasury.

The high level of detail dedicated to these areas demonstrates the remarkable organisation and centralisation of the state idealised in the *Arthaśāstra*. It also supports the view that the information contained in the text is a compilation of works that have endured over long periods of trial and error. The *Arthaśāstra* is surprisingly calculated on every minute detail and economic function—the exact number of *panas* is provided for every salaried position, legal ramification, commodity, and livestock. Economics was regulated through such central planning and the highly detailed attempts at identifying the optimal amount for every economic function stresses this constant strive towards efficiently improving the overall utility and welfare of society.

The coin most often mentioned in the *Arthaśāstra* is the *pana*. The value of a *pana* has been calculated in relation to the cost of living. An annual salary of 60 *panas* could be substituted by an *adhaka* of grain per day, enough for four meals for one *Arya* male. It is also mentioned in the text that the cash wage was 5 *panas* a month for the lowest paid. The *pana* was indeed a valuable coin.

Along with prudence and careful calculation, the state is advised to be extremely active or energetic in managing the economy, as the *Arthaśāstra* states that "the root of material well-being is activity, of material disaster its reverse. In the absence of activity, there is certain destruction of what is obtained and of what is not yet received. By activity reward is obtained, and one also secures abundance of riches."

However, despite the many readily offered solutions and suggestions in the *Arthaśāstra*, the application of such principles was far from being an easy task, which is why the king depended heavily on his councillors. It was the latter who comprised the strategic and intellectual leadership of the state.

Effective intelligence would allow a state to carefully weigh the odds of foreign and domestic policy measures, and skilfully apply the principles underlying the text. Intelligence was the prerequisite for applying strategy, internally through a secret service or externally through espionage and psychological warfare. The *Arthaśāstra* cherishes strategic means for achieving political and economic ends because of its inherent efficiency—strategy meant leverage. It mentions that a single assassin can achieve, with weapons, fire or poison, more than a fully mobilised army. The presumably large scale of the state economy idealised in the *Arthaśāstra* necessitated abundant use of covert operations in order to defend the state against external threats and quell internal dissension.

The rapid growth and centralisation of states seemed to have greatly reduced the margin for error in government policies and measures undertaken. The *Arthaśāstra* warns of several instances in which seemingly minor mistakes may precipitate the entire collapse of the state, and conversely, the text also advocates methods to engineer similar stratagems on enemy states through covert operations. As an example, in several cases the *Arthaśāstra* recommends the use of young women of great beauty, or courtesans, to seduce and become intimate with rival military leaders and political officials so as to set the stage for provoking quarrels amongst them or inducing assassination. The honey-trap is thus an ancient method of espionage or political killing. Similarly, deceptive means are undertaken to ensure loyalty and immediately quell any dissension within the state. The text even advocates the continual testing of the king's own councillors in order to determine their proficiency in *dharma*, *artha*, and *kama*, as well as having secret agents test the loyalties of queens and princes by trying to tempt them to overthrow the king.

To defend against these stratagems from rival states, ironically, the *Arthaśāstra* advocates steadfast adherence to religion. It states that, in times past, kings had perished because they fell prey to one or other of the six vices (lust, anger, greed, conceit, arrogance and foolhardiness) and that the aggressor was in danger of following these kings who had no self-control. It was better to pay heed to spiritual and material well-being (*dharma* and *artha*). Those who advised him to behave rashly, in violation of the principles of *dharma* and *artha*, were friends only in name but were really his enemies.

These weaknesses or deviations from religious principles were also tested amongst the general populace by secret agents. The text identifies individuals departing from the practice of *dharma* as the most likely sources of opposition to the state. The rationale behind this religious self-control and moderation urged by the *Arthaśāstra* may be likened to how skilled poker players are trained to control their emotions and think strategically amidst high-pressure situations. Hence, religion was taken as an effective buffer against external and internal strategic threats and the strong adherence to it was essential for ultimately outmanoeuvring enemy states.

The *Arthaśāstra* delves into strategic thinking in India in ancient times and attempts to give it a contemporary interpretation. Its basic advantage is the written text as opposed to oral tradition in India. There is also a strong religious base of Indian thought. An off-shoot of the religious element in India was the social organisation it produced. Warfare in India was almost exclusively the preserve and even the duty of the *kshatriya varna* (warrior class) which was hereditary, although specific instances of the priestly *brahmin varna* can be found thinking about and engaging in warfare.

A strong school of *realpolitik* also appeared in India side by side with it. Thus, ancient Indian thinkers produced two schools of war, diplomacy and interstate relations; the *dharmayuddha* (ethical warfare) school; and the *kutayuddha* (devious warfare) school. The two schools were, however, not mutually exclusive. The practitioners of each school were influenced by the principles and methods of the other and practised them. The best example of this is the great Mahabharata war in which one can see both schools of thought in operation: in this war the victory went to the practitioners of the *kutayuddha* school although the war itself has always been described as *dharmayuddha*. In the other epic war, the Ramayana, although both streams of thought were at work, victory went to the *dharmayuddha* (righteous/ethical) school. At the level of rhetoric, the concept of *dharmayuddha* always reigned supreme. But in practice *kutayuddha* was often the norm. The defeat of Indian kings at the hands of foreign conquerors has been attributed by many to the loss of traditions of war-making, particularly that of *kutayuddha*. This is probably why, at present in modern India, the *kutayuddha* school seems to be in the ascendant, although even there the righteousness of the cause always dominates the rhetoric.

Shaurya (heroism) continued to be valued as the virtue of an individual warrior but to this was added the concept of *neeti* (ethical principles) in the conduct of warfare. The belief grew that without *neeti*, war became merely a display of animal-like ferocity. For a victory based on principles (*dharmavijaya*), the king and the warriors had to observe certain codes in warfare.

These codes were incorporated in the *Dharmashastras* (loosely translated as Books of Law). Warfare carried out according to the codes was also called *prakashayudha* (illuminated or open warfare). There was nothing secret about it. Preparations for such a war were made openly in the full knowledge of the adversary. There was no element of surprise and there were strict rules about seasons of warfare, the duration of combat was restricted to daylight hours and rigid codes about close combat between warriors were observed. In all this, there was no room for strategy or tactics; only the numbers of warriors, their skills and the quality of weaponry counted. But, at the same time, diplomacy played an important role in building alliances for war and in making decisions about whether or not to go to war.

Inevitably, in actual warfare, the principles of righteous warfare were often set aside by individual warriors or their commanders. In fact, such was the sweetness of victory that some kings waged war for reasons of self-aggrandizement. The victory achieved for such selfish reasons came to be classified into two categories: *asuravijaya* in which the enemy's territory was annexed, enemy kings and commanders were punished after the war, enemy cities were destroyed and the women were carried away as war booty. The second category produced *lobhavijaya* or victory out of covetousness or greed. This did not need waging a ruthless war of destruction but one for gain in terms of territory, wealth, women and so forth.

Only *kutayuddha* (devious warfare) could produce victories aimed at self-aggrandizement, Although the form was repeatedly denounced by ancient sages, it was nevertheless practised with increasing frequency, and came to be accepted as a norm. From practice, codification of devious warfare was only a short step. But a comprehensive codification was undertaken by Kautilya in the *Arthaśāstra*. The term *kuta*, in the context of hunting, was used for a trap or snare. Consequently, in the context of warfare, it came to mean ensnaring or trapping the enemy. This included the use of magic spells and such other occult methods. And when it came to weaponry prevalent in those days, it included the use of poisoned arrows, fire arrows and such other unauthorised weapons which could bring about destruction of men and property on a large scale. Other methods included poisoning of the enemy's water sources, attack by stealth, enticing the enemy into an unfavourable position, bribery, assassinations and attacks at night.

Almost every single war described in the epics and the *puranas* incorporated at least some of these forbidden methods. Sometimes, only one side is said to have done this. In the Ramayana, for example, the *rakhsasa* side is said to have resorted to *kuta* methods. In the numerous wars fought between the *devas* and *asuras* the latter are always accused of having used unethical methods. In general, it seems that such methods were attributed to the side which was technologically superior but nevertheless lost the series of wars in the end. The didactic message of these classics was that righteousness always emerged victorious. A few epics like the *Agni Purana*, however, condoned the use of *kuta* methods by the weak as a last resort.

One prominent characteristic of the Hindu reading of reality is that good is always mixed with or accompanied by evil. Human nature is the product of a variety of influences (*karma*) from previous births and the present life. Thus, the same human being contains both righteous and unrighteous impulses, and even the most ideally righteous person may occasionally commit unethical acts in the interests of larger righteous causes. Thus, in the Ramayana, Lord Rama, the most perfect human being known nevertheless kills Vali, a brother of his ally, by deceit. In the Mahabharata, Lord Krishna, himself a major God in the Hindu pantheon, advises and resorts to all kinds of trickery in the service of the weak, but righteous side, in a dispute over a kingdom. Hindu classics always uphold the rhetoric of righteousness or *dharma* but condone and often justify lapses from the codes.

Kautilya, who rose as a strategic thinker in a period of constant warfare; realised the importance of studying war as an important aspect of statecraft. In the *Arthaśāstra* , he recommends that a state should base its defences on the fort (*durg*) and the army. Of the two, he regards the fort to be more important since it allows the king to survive a siege and practise his diplomacy from that base. The army is, of course, important in defence matters but it can be completely lost on the battlefield leaving the king without any protection.

For the defence of the state against enemies, the *Arthaśāstra* prescribes at least four bases, one each in every cardinal direction. These should preferably be natural defensive points such as mountains, water, desert, forests and the like. But in the state capital, a man-made fort is regarded as essential. It should have moats, ramparts and parapets for soldiers to shoot from. Wooden walls are ruled out as a fire-hazard. In the approaches to the fort, traps should be laid for the enemy. Inside it, it should be guarded by four types of formations comprising elephants, chariots, cavalry and infantry, each led by several commanders so that the loss of one or more to the enemy does not leave the formations leaderless. The fort should, of course, be well-stocked to withstand a siege but should have secret escape routes if the situation became desperate.

The troops should, naturally, be from the warrior castes as far as possible. Lower *varna* are acceptable but the highest *varna*, the Brahmins, are ruled out because of the peculiar Indian social system. Kautilya avers that the enemy can put Brahmin troops out of action simply by prostrating before them and prostrating persons, by law, could not be killed. The infantry can be a standing force or it can be raised for the particular war. But other branches, e.g., elephants, cavalry etc., must be standing formations led and trained by specialists. The army of an ally can be used but captured enemy soldiers should be used only with caution.

The *Arthaśāstra* prescribes a detailed hierarchy of officers. The *Senapati* or commander-in-chief is the highest officer, his station is at the rear. The lower commanders (*nayakas*) actually lead the troops in battle. Daily rigorous training must be the norm. Frequent inspections are required to keep the troops fighting fit. As for weapons, there should be a special office for acquiring them and storing them safely. Each weapon is to be marked with the king's insignia and strict inventories must be maintained to guard against loss.

Three main types of weapons are prescribed and seem actually to have been maintained in ordnance depots. The first category consisted of battlefield weapons such as bows and arrows, spears, swords, daggers, shields etc. The second type comprises those for defence of the fort such as stones, catapults and bows and arrows. The third type is meant for attacking enemy fortifications which includes scaling equipment as well as flaming arrows and other incendiary weapons. The *Arthaśāstra* puts a great deal of faith in magical practices such as casting spells.

In Kautilya's time, warfare was limited only to certain seasons. Generally it was avoided during the rainy season. The *Arthaśāstra* generally upholds this practice but stresses that the time for launching a war should also depend on the terrain which would become the battlefield. It also prescribes that the type of troops to be deployed should be determined not only by the terrain but also by the disposition of enemy troops. It also lays down elaborate rules for establishing camps during the march against an enemy.

Although the *Arthaśāstra* puts a great deal of emphasis on devious warfare (*kutayuddha*), it prescribes that if a king has a clearly superior force and other factors are favourable, he should engage in open and rule-bound warfare (*prakashayudha*). Obviously in Kautilya's mind, a certain amount of odium continued to be associated with devious warfare. For it involved among other things attacking the enemy when he was vulnerable, feigning retreat to draw out the enemy into a trap, using elephants to break up closed ranks, attacking one flank and then the other, tiring out the enemy with one's inferior troops first and then attacking with superior ones, laying ambushes, attacking at night to deprive enemy soldiers of their sleep and then attacking them during the day with fresh troops, attacking the enemy troops when they were facing the sun and so forth. All such tactics are routine now but they were regarded as exceptional in Kautilya's time.

The *Arthaśāstra* also goes into great detail about the conventional warfare of its time. It prescribes standard battle formations or arrays (*vyuha*) which have a centre, two flanks and two wings. Each component of the *vyuha* is conceived as being of equal strength containing between 9 and 21 units; each unit in turn, being based on an elephant or a chariot with five horsemen and 15 infantrymen in front and rear. There are four basic types of battle-arrays: the staff (in-line) array, the serpent (wavy) array, the circular array and the loose army. The choice is determined by the terrain and the enemy's troop disposition.

Great emphasis is placed on reserves behind every battle-array; where the king stations himself. The *Arthaśāstra* shows preference for mountains or forts to station the reserves. With the reserve force, there should be physicians and medicaments to treat the wounded, and field kitchens run by women. The women are also trusted with the task of 'encouraging' the troops.

Before the beginning of action, the king should address his troops and emphasize that he is one of them. Next the commander-in-chief (*senapati*) should also address them and announce rewards for acts of bravery. (For example, killing the enemy king earned the reward of 10,000 *panas* and there were lesser rewards for other acts). Whatever loot the soldiers captured would be theirs and the Chief should also announce gratuities at the end of the war. It was the task of the officers to report acts of bravery by men fighting under their charge.

Whatever the form of warfare, the *Arthaśāstra* is scrupulous about one principle: not to cause harm to the subjects of the enemy king. Thus, when laying a siege to the fort, the people inside must be assured of safety and allowed to leave the fort for safer places, after the fort is captured. If territory must be annexed—it was usually not annexed—only the king was forced to become an ally or a vassal, and the people are to be won over through other means. Their customs must be respected and their gods must be revered by the new king. After the war, carrying away loot is forbidden. If the king was reduced to vassalage, he was still permitted to retain control of the territory and the army and was not obliged to help its sovereign militarily.

It needs to be emphasised that the *Arthaśāstra* does not only speak about making conquests. It also discusses the strategies and tactics for the prevention of conquest by others. This is why a large portion of the book is devoted to statecraft and administration of the state. But whether in conquering others or in preventing conquest, the *Arthaśāstra* takes a conflictual relationship between states as the norm. Therefore, management of these occupies an important place in Kautilya's thinking. It is almost certain that a large number of ideas he propounds came to him as received wisdom. And after him these ideas were appropriated by different texts as their own.

The *Arthaśāstra* envisages the "international" arena, the *mandala*, as comprising 12 types of kings/states. It classifies them as follows:

1. The would-be conqueror, at the centre of the *mandala*.
2. The enemy whose territory borders on that of the would-be conqueror, i.e., the hostile neighbour.
3. The ally's whose territory lies immediately beyond that of the hostile neighbour.
4. The enemy's ally who is the neighbour of one's won ally.
5. The ally's ally who is territorially distant.
6. The ally of the enemy's ally who is also territorially distant.

Types 7 to 10 follow the same sequence, but are to the rear of the would-be conqueror. The last two types are No. 11, a neutral king/ state neighbouring both the would-be conqueror and his/its enemy but is stronger than both. And 12, the king who is totally indifferent towards all other kings/states but is more powerful than the would-be conqueror, his enemy and the neutral king/ state.

All the advice in the *Arthaśāstra* is directed to the would-be conqueror (*vijigisu* or one desirous of victory). The underlying assumption is that neighbours always turn hostile. Another assumption is that a common enemy creates allies. But the categories of enemy and ally are not fixed. Under certain conditions, allies can become friends and vice-versa. The 12 types classified by the *Arthaśāstra* are possible combinations; they are not to be taken as the permanently existing situation in a *mandala*. Kautilya assumes that except for the neutral and 'indifferent' kings/ states, all others in the *mandala* are of equal strength. Therefore, in a concrete situation, the *mandala* gets divided into two more or less equal blocs, with one bloc's leader seeking to establish hegemony over all the others. The strengths of blocs being equal, diplomacy, strategy and tactics assume great importance attaining hegemony.

The *Arthaśāstra* emphasize the role of diplomacy but shows no preference for it over war. This is simply because one important component of the society of his time was the warrior group whose very existence was tied to fighting. Diplomacy, Kautilya was for winning allies, delaying war if one was vulnerable and for making post-war arrangements for a new order.

According to the *Arthaśāstra*, relations with other kings/states are to be established and carried out through *dutas* or ambassadors. It prescribes three types of ambassadors: the plenipotentiary, an envoy with limited negotiating powers, and one who is only a messenger. It recommends that ambassadors should be stationed in all foreign states on a permanent basis and that they should enjoy what we call 'diplomatic immunity'. In contrast to modern diplomatic norms, however, the *Arthaśāstra* expects the ambassadors to engage in espionage, acts of sabotage and most importantly be active in securing defections from the enemy's army.

Kautilya distinguished between six major approaches to foreign policy. The first is a policy of maintaining peace with another state which is based on a treaty detailing the terms and conditions. The second is the policy of hostility which should be followed if one is stronger than the enemy. The third approach is one of inaction, which is most suitable when states are of equal strength. The fourth is outright invasion but this policy is recommended for the very strong. For the very weak is prescribed a fifth approach, i.e., seeking shelter with another king and waiting for better days, The sixth and the last approach recommends a policy of peace with one king/state while maintaining hostility towards another; such a dual policy is possible if help is available from another state to fight the enemy.

The *Arthaśāstra*, naturally realizes that one may become the object of such policies by another king/state and the enemy may force peace by a treaty. If that happens, Kautilya advises that one should drag one's feet in fulfilling the treaty obligations and wait for an opportunity to overthrow the enemy. If the treaty demands a hostage, for example, one should offer an inferior person. But if the enemy demands one's son as a hostage, the king should offer himself so that the son can plan to overthrow the enemy and rescue the father.

The *Arthaśāstra* describes many kinds of treaties, with or without various stipulations, temporary and long-term ones, sincere and dishonest ones. The aim is always to outsmart the adversary. It also discusses in great detail not only the six broad approaches outlined but also their combinations. Even the necessity of surrender is not overlooked but it is always for buying time.

War-making is only one among the means to attain one's objective of hegemony. The other means are friendship or bribery against weak kings. Other two means which could be employed against the strong are splitting the enemy's strength and alliances), and coercion (which includes war). The difference between the means and approaches/policies is that the means can be employed against domestic as well as foreign opponents whereas policies can apply only to other kings/states.

By way of broad strategy, the *Arthaśāstra* recommends that the would-be conqueror should first proceed against the hostile neighbour and, with the newly-acquired power, he should next tackle the neutral king/state. If he succeeds, he should proceed against the most powerful or 'indifferent' king. That would complete his hegemony over the *mandala* as a whole, for the rest would fall in line. if there are no neutral or "indifferent" kings, the conqueror should first tackle his enemies and then secure the allegiance of enemy's allies. In the event there are only two other states, one hostile and the other friendly, the would-be conqueror should crush the neighbouring state regardless of whether it is hostile or friendly and then proceed against the other. Finally, if there are a number of neighbouring states, they should be tackled one by one gaining strength in the process.

It goes without saying that Kautilya underlines all his strategies with the requirement that the would-be conqueror must satisfy himself that he enjoys superiority in such essential aspects as troop morale, war materiel and above all strategic advice. At the same time, the king must take precautions against insurrection within his own kingdom while he is away at war. So the *Arthaśāstra* recommends that a reliable Regent should be appointed and one-third of the army left behind for internal security. The most likely rebel leader should be taken by the king on his expedition. The *Arthaśāstra* , as may be expected, also discusses how an insurrection should be planned and executed. Finally, it elaborately discusses how gains and losses from an expedition against others should be estimated beforehand.

Kautilya wrote a practical handbook and therefore does not indulge in any theory of a good society, good actions etc. This is why to the modern mind he comes across as a totally amoral and cynical practitioner of strategies for war. Most Western comment on the *Arthaśāstra* is therefore negative in the extreme. In India, however, the book has never evoked any such negative response. This seems largely because despite the odium attached to *kutayuddha*, in all epic wars, the righteous side always emerged victorious. *Kutayuddha* always remained a kind of side-show. The second reason is that the *Arthaśāstra* was appropriated by other *shastras* and the *puranas* (or epics) in which the moral/ethical side of all human actions was abundantly stressed; so, devious and cynical practices came to be considered secondary, situational and answering only the needs of exigencies.

Kautilya make it abundantly clear that war is much more than just a fight among men: reliance on sheer military power does not assure victory. What we today call 'software' is much more important than the 'hardware'. Thus strategy and tactics become supremely important elements to be practised in tandem with diplomacy.

Kautilya was a great practitioner of *realpolitik*. He did not indulge in moralising or theorising about the ends of power. Beyond a concession to righteous principles, his attention was focussed on the goal: the achievement of victory through any means appropriate for the occasion. These include obtaining accurate information about the enemy's plans and actions to frustrate them. He strongly advocated measures to break up the enemy's alliances and his internal structure in order to isolate and demoralize him. He recommended indirect and devious approaches with deception at all levels playing the central role. However, despite such single-mindedness in achieving victory/hegemony, Kautilya did express concern about minimising the economic costs of war as well as minimising civilian causalities.

Despite the great similarities between the ideas of Sun Tzu and Kautilya, there remains one major difference which has to do with the different social systems of India and China. Sun Tzu's thinking may be summed up as: "the greatest victory is one where the enemy is subdued without fighting." Such a sweeping doctrine would have been inconceivable for Kautilya because that would have devalued the entire hereditary warrior *varna*. For this class, it was a disgrace to die anywhere except on the battlefield. So, a world without war was even theoretically inconceivable to Kautilya.

The *Arthaśāstra* is the key text on Indian strategic culture, based entirely on the role of power. For Kautilya power was the means and not the end. "Strength is power, and happiness is the end. [...] Hence a king shall always endeavour to augment his own power and elevate his happiness". For the augmentation of power the general rule applies that "whoever is inferior to another shall make peace with him; whoever is superior in power shall wage war" so power was the basis for the acquisition of more power.

The Indian independence movement needed Kautilya vis-à-vis the colonial power in order to demonstrate that the ancient *Arthaśāstra* was at par with, or even superior to, the ancient and medieval works of European political theory. However, after Independence, Kautilya appeared to have been discarded. There was much ambiguity in national policy consisting of an opaque mix of idealism and Kautilyan *realpolitik.* India's political leadership was predominantly idealist and the nation has had to pay a high price in its wars since then. However, India has been on a learning curve through which, slowly but steadily, the relative weight of the "Kautilya factor" has increased in her strategic stance.

In matters of foreign policy, Chanakya considered international politics to be anarchical and expected the rule by the strongest in an ever unstable environment where empires either expanded or declined, but rarely stood still. On the domestic front, Kautilya's insistence on clear and just laws that must be backed by force are a clear warning of the perils of internal anarchy and strife.

Kautilya advised the king to break with tradition only if doing so enhanced national security. He argued that national interest should override moral principles inasmuch the moral order depends upon the continued existence of the state. Yet, Kautilya never advocated the conquest of lands outside of South Asia. This line of thought is still visible in modern Indian foreign policy: contrary to virtually all other major powers, India has never taken the initiative to invade a foreign country, and it has never shown interest in areas beyond South Asia.

Kautilya's most significant contribution to foreign policy making remains his '*mandala* theory'; according to which one's immediate neighbours are enemies, while states on the other side of one's neighbours are friends. In many cases, this theory seems correct, for example when trying to explain China's warm ties with Pakistan. And interestingly enough, India's relationship with its immediate neighbours have been historically bad. Today, India's major challenge is to turn her immediate neighbours into friends and foster regional integration.

Even ages after his death, the ideas propounded by Chanakya are still alive in the political scene of India which is proof of his great political acumen. It shows that he was successful in developing the science of politics as he had aspired to do, and we see his principles being used by the political scientists and defence analysts of today.

THE LIFE OF CHANAKYA

Chanakya (c. 350-283 B.C.) was an adviser and Prime Minister to the first Maurya Emperor Chandragupta (c. 340-293 B.C.) and is regarded as the architect of his early rise to power. His actual name is believed to be Vishnugupta. To many he was known as Kautilya but to most he was known as Chānakya , the son of Chanak, the most renowned teacher in Magadha. The *Arthashastra* identifies its author by the name of Kautilya, except for one verse which refers to him by the name of Vishnugupta.

One of the earliest Sanskrit writing to explicitly identify Chanakya with Vishnugupta was Vishnu Sarma's *Panchatantra*, written in the 3rd century B.C. Chanakya is considered a pioneer in the field of economics and diplomacy. He was a teacher at the Takshashila University and is widely believed to be responsible for the creation of the Mauryan Empire, the first empire on the Indian subcontinent.

There are several versions regarding the birth of Chanakya. According to the Jaina version, he was born in the village of Chanak to a Brahmin couple. The Pali version says that he was a Brahmin from Takshila. There is also a claim that he belonged to a Brahmin group from modern day Kerala. Chanakya was tutored extensively in the Vedas which he is said to have memorised at a very early age. He was also believed to have studied mathematics, geography, the legal systems of those times and science (including astronomy and *ayurveda*) along with religion.

His father, the revered *Acharya* Chanak, had been beheaded by Dhanananda, the despotic ruler of Magadha, in a fit of rage.

As a consequence, the young Vishnugupta is said to have taken the name of Chānakya (son of Chanak) to remind him always of the circumstances of his father's death which led him to flee from Pataliputra. He travelled to Takshashila (Taxila), where he became a teacher of politics. Takshashila was linked through the northern high road of commerce (*uttarapatha*) along the base of the Himalayas to the kingdom of Magadha with its capital city, Pataliputra, (now known as Patna).

The Greek invasion into India during that time caused widespread political turmoil in North-West India. The ruler of Taxila and Gandhara, Ambhi, signed a treaty with Alexander and acquiesced in the latter's incursion across the Hindu Kush mountains. Chanakya viewed the foreign invasion as an intrusion against Indian culture and sought other local rulers and advocated them to unite and fight Alexander. Porus was the only king who challenged Alexander at the Battle of the Hydaspes, but was defeated. This forced Chanakya to leave the university environment and return to Pataliputra which was still ruled by the Nanda King, Dhanananda.

Although Chanakya initially prospered in his relations with the ruler, but being a blunt and outspoken individual, he soon fell from grace when he tried to point out to Dhanananda the errors of his despotic and profligate rule. It led to Chanakya being removed from his official position in the court. In the Chanakya legend, it is mentioned that he was insulted and thrown out of the Nanda court by the King Dhanananda, whereupon he swore revenge. Legend also has it that Chanakya took an oath to leave his long tuft of hair on the top or on the back of his shaven head (*sikha*) unknotted or untied until he had succeeded in humbling the debauched Nanda kings and removing them from power.

Though Chanakya was just a professor in the Taxila University which seemed to be far away from the happenings in the rest of the country, he actually was able to influence the rulers in a big way. His students looked at him as an ideal teacher who inspired and exemplified great sagacity and knowledge. His students respected him and were ready to fight at any moment on his orders. Two of his students, who have been mentioned at various instances, were Bhadrabhatt and Purushdutt. In the events that unfolded in the life of Chanakya, these two played a pivotal role towards the achievement of his goals. It is believed that they acted as spies for Chanakya, collecting information about his enemies.

During his travels, Chānakya met Chandragupta, the future emperor, by happenstance and found in him a kindred spirit and the perfect foil to overthrow the Nanda regime in Magadha. Chandragupta was the grandson of king Sarvarthasiddhi, who had two wives, Sunandadevi and Muradevi. Sunanda begat nine sons called the Navanandas. Mura had only one, Chandragupta's father. The Nandas of Magadha eliminated most of the Sarvarthasiddhi clan. Chandragupta survived along with his mother by taking refuge in a forest, but the circumstances of his life caused him to be distraught and fill up with a desire for revenge against the Nanda rulers. (Chandragupta's father, although a mere *dasiputra*, i.e. the son of a maidservant, had converted to Buddhism). They lived in an area where there were large flock of peacocks (*mor*), hence his adoption of the appellation of Maurya. Chanakya, freshly insulted by the Nandas (there were four Nanda brothers, with Dhanananda as the ruler) found a companion to destroy the king and get Chandragupta his rightful place as king of Patliputra. From then on Chanakya and Chandragupta worked in tandem to destroy the corrupt and unscrupulous rule of the Nandas.

Chandragupta was highly intelligent, courageous and physically powerful. Chanakya was impressed by the young man's personality and mien, and immediately took him under his wings. Both of them travelled back to Takshashila where Chānakya took charge of his education and training for kingship. He began sowing the seeds of the dream of building an empire that could protect the Indian territories from foreign invasion into his disciple. Both began laying the foundation of the future Maurya Empire. Chanakya cared little for the fact that due to his low birth (i.e., being a *dasiputra*) Chandragupta could not approach the throne or become the ruler. A man of immense discretion, Chanakya's desire was that only a ruler of extraordinary capabilities should be raised to the exalted position of ruling Magadha, so that the expansion of the Greeks could be repulsed.

A story, perhaps apocryphal, is part of the Chānakya legend relating to his final selection of Chandragupta to conqueror the Magadha Empire from King Dhanananda. Chānakya already had a disciple, a princeling named Prabhudutt or Pabbato. On taking Chandragupta under his tutelage he encircled his neck with a single fold of woollen cord, twisted with golden thread. He invested Prabhudutt also, with a similar woollen cord. While these youths were living with him, each had a dream which they separately imparted to him. As soon as he heard each dream he knew that, of the two, Chandragupta would become paramount monarch in Magadha. However, he disclosed nothing to them but decided on a further test.

On a certain occasion during their travels, retiring from the main road, and lying down in a shady place protected by the deep foliage of trees, they fell asleep. The *Acharya* awaking first rose and, for the purpose of putting Prabhudutt to the test, gave him a sword and told him to bring the woollen thread on Chandragupta's neck, without either cutting or untying it. The disciple failed to accomplish it and returned. On a subsequent day, he sent Chandragupta on a similar mission. Repairing to the spot where the disciple was sleeping, and considering how it was to be effected, decided that there is no way of doing it without cutting his head off. Accordingly chopping his head off, he brought the woollen cord to Chānakya , who received it in profound silence. Chānakya , from that time, knew that he had an ardent pupil who deserved kingship.

Chanakya and Chandragupta formed alliances with other rulers and invaded the inhabited parts of the Magadha Empire. They were initially rebuffed by the forces of King Dhanananda. Another apocryphal story relates that Chānakya overheard a woman chiding her son who had burnt his tongue while eating hot food from his plate. She admonished the child and directed him to eat from the sides first rather than put his spoon in the centre of the plate. Drawing a lesson from this they began operations by nibbling Magadha territory from unguarded frontiers.

In order to defeat the Nandas, Chanakya had to employ various strategies. He first tested the policy of attacking the core of the city but met with a string of defeats. Change their strategy, Chanakya and Chandragupta began attacks on the borders of the Magadha Empire. Again there were mistakes. The troops were not stationed in the areas conquered. So when they marched ahead, the people of the conquered areas joined together again and encircled their army. Thus those who had been defeated had to be fought again. Chandragupta and Chanakya learnt lessons from these mistakes and stationed troops in the conquered regions so that the enemy could not resurrect and cause further trouble.

Chanakya with his cleverness had earlier won the friendship of king Parvataka (Porus). Parvataka, his brother Vairochaka and son Malayeketu came with their armies to help them. The Nanda king had a large army as well as important support and guidance of his very able minister, Amatya Rakshasa, who had great loyalty towards the king. Chanakya knew that getting Amatya out of his way was the only way of defeating King Nanda. Accordingly, he devised a plan which involved planting of spies in the enemy camp. In a very short span of time, the weaknesses of the Nandas became visible.

It was a keen and bitter fight. In the ensuing war, Chandragupta faced off against Bhadrashala, the commander of the King Dhanananda's army and was eventually able to defeat him in a series of battle, that ended with the siege of the capital city Pataliputra and the conquest of the Nanda Empire around 321 B.C; thus laying the foundations of the powerful 'Maurya Empire' in Northern India by the time he was about 20 years old. The Nanda king was banished and all relatives and sons were killed, once Amatya Rakshasa was rendered helpless. Chandragupta was victorious proving the foresight of Chanakya regarding his abilities. The Nanda king and his wife retired to the forest. It is said that after sometime Chanakya had both of them killed, because he thought that if Amatya Rakshasa made them take a son by the rights of adoption, there would be claimants to the throne. He wanted the lineage of the Nandas totally eliminated.

After the downfall of the Nanda dynasty, it was not difficult for Chandragupta to win the support of the citizens of Magadha, who responded warmly to their new young ruler. The rulers of the neighbouring states rallied under Chandragupta's suzerainty and the last of the Greeks headed by Alexander's general, Seleucus were defeated. It is believed that Chandragupta had established himself so firmly in the Punjab that when, in 306 or 305 B.C., Seleucus I Nicator crossed the river Indus in an endeavour to recover the erstwhile provinces conquered by Alexander the Great, he found the Mauryan Emperor confronting him with such formidable force that he was constrained to make peace on terms wholly in favour of the Mauryan Emperor. Under those terms, Seleucus not only acknowledged Emperor Chandragupta's sovereignty over the Punjab and Gandhara, he also ceded to him parts of other provinces, while he himself received only 500 elephants in return. This treaty was sealed by a matrimonial alliance between the two royal houses with Seleucus giving a daughter or niece in marriage to the Emperor Chandragupta or, possibly, to his son Bindusara.

With the dual obstacles of the Nandas and Greek forces out of the way, Chanakya used every political device and intrigue to unite the greater portion of the Indian subcontinent. Under his guidance, Emperor Chandragupta Maurya conquered all the lands up to Iran in the North West and down to the extremities of the Mysore State in the South; from the Himalayas on the North to Burma on the East. Pataliputra was the capital city. It was by his wits alone that the austere and ascetic Brahman, Chanakya, directed the formation of the greatest Indian Empire ever seen in history.

Although many great savants of the science of *niti* such as Brihaspati, Shukracharya, Bhartrihari and Vishnusharma have

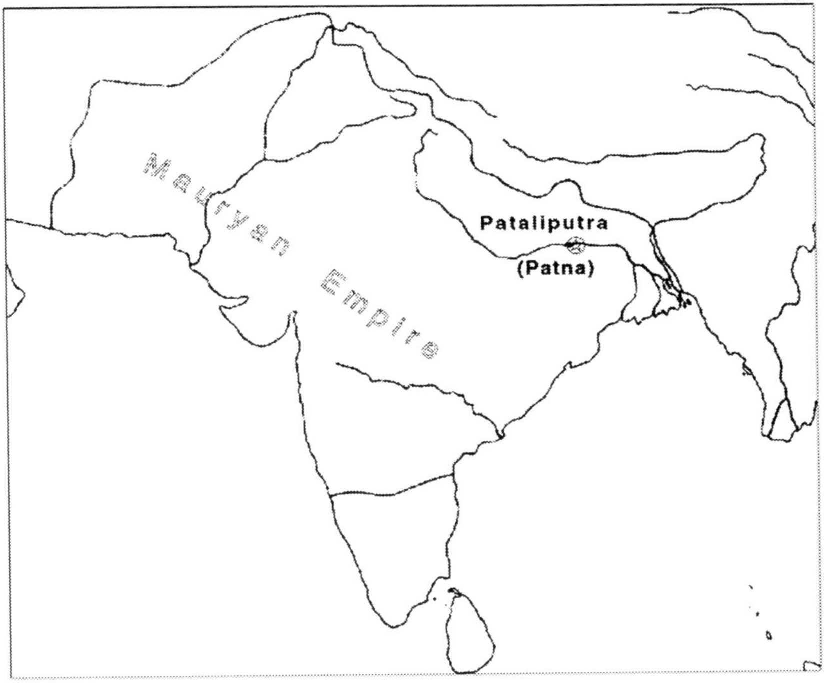

Map showing the Mauryan Empire

imparted instructions in their own celebrated works, it is perhaps the way that Chanakya applied his teachings of *nitisastra* that has made him stand out as a significant historical figure. The major lesson that Chānakya imparts is that lofty ideals can become a reality if we intelligently work towards achieving our goal in a determined, progressive and practical manner. Two books are attributed to Chanakya—*Arthashastra* and *Nitisastra* which is also known as Chanakya *Niti*. The latter is a treatise on the ideal way of living.

According to a legend, (which is perhaps a later Jaina invention) it is believed that while Chanakya served as the Prime Minister of Chandragupta Maurya, he started adding small quantities of poison in Chandragupta's food—so that he would get used to it and develop resistance to poison. The aim was to prevent the Emperor from being poisoned by enemies. One day the Queen, Durdha, shared a meal with the Emperor (the Queen was in the family way then). Since she was not used to eating poisoned food, she died. Chanakya was determined that the baby should not die; therefore, he cut open the belly of the dead Queen and took out the baby. A drop (*bindu*) of her poisoned blood had touched the baby's head, and hence Chanakya named him Bindusara. Bindusara later went on to become a great Emperor in his own right and also fathered the greatest Mauryan Emperor since Chandragupta—Emperor Asoka.

Later on, Chandragupta Maurya converted to Jainism. In true Hindu tradition Chānakya is said to have persuaded the Emperor to forsake his throne, and take *sanyasa* (retirement from life). Chandragupta renounced the throne and followed the Jain saint Bhadrabahu to present day Karnataka and settled in a place known as Shravana Belagola where he did prolonged meditation and finally achieved *moksha*. He lived as an ascetic for some years and died due to voluntary starvation, according to the Jain tradition.

Chanakya meanwhile stayed on as the Prime Minister of the second Mauryan Emperor, Bindusara. Bindusara also had another minister named Subandhu who did not like Chanakya. One day, he told Bindusara that Chanakya was responsible for the death (murder) of his mother. Bindusara inquired the facts from the nurses who confirmed this, thereby causing him to turn against Chanakya.

It is said that Chanakya, on hearing that Emperor Bindusara was incensed with him, thought that he was in any case at the end of his life. He donated all his wealth and possessions to the poor, widows and orphans and sat on a dung heap, prepared to die by total abstinence from food and drink. Bindusara meanwhile heard the full story of his birth from the nurses and rushed to beg forgiveness from Chanakya. But Chanakya did not relent. Thereafter, Bindusara vent his fury on Subandhu, who asked for time to seek forgiveness from Chanakya. However Subandhu, who still hated Chanakya, wanted to make sure that he (Chanakya) would not return to the city. Therefore, he arranged for a ceremony of respect, but unnoticed by anyone, slipped a smouldering charcoal ember inside the dung heap (on which Chanakya was seated). Aided by the wind, the dung heap swiftly caught fire, and the man who laid the foundation of the Maurya Empire and authored the ancient Indian treatise on statecraft, economic policy and military strategy—*Arthaśāstra*—was burnt to death. Chanakya passed away around 283 B.C.

Chanakya's two main philosophies were, "A debt should be paid off till the last penny" and "An enemy should be destroyed without a trace." Ironically, Subandhu too followed the same philosophies in order to destroy him. Thus was the very tragic end of this political, economic and military genius.

The momentous life of Chanakya is a saga where an individual is obsessed by the idea of revenge. However, personal revenge was not the aim of Chanakya. He wanted the kingdom to be secure and that its administration should bring happiness to the people. He thought that there were two ways of ensuring the happiness of the people. It is possible that, while he spent time with Chandragupta, during the latter's period of *sanyas*, he began the task of writing the *Arthaśāstra*.

Chanakya, perhaps, is the only personality who has been accepted and revered as a genius both by Indian and Western scholars. His life is a historical milestone in the making of India amidst tremendous upheavals and myriad's of reversals. Celebrated as a shrewd statesman and a ruthless administrator, he comes across as one the greatest diplomats of the world. He had the courage to speak his heart out even in front of the rulers, which shows his strong inclination to democratic values and the audacity to put his views through. Although, he lived around the 3rd century BC, his ideas and principles show concurrence and validity in the present day world. Politics was his forte. Diplomacy in a politically charged environment shows his self-confidence and the ability to stay calm in trying situations. His foresight and wide knowledge coupled with politics of expediency founded the mighty Mauryan Empire in India. He was a great laureate of economics with a glittering intellect to perceive the intricate dynamics of the various economic activities and principles.

The contents of the *Arthaśāstra* display the distinct effects of his thoughts on the way a kingdom is managed and other facets of economic administration. Even today, one of his maxims on taxation is very much alive and calls for adherence by the governments of the world. According to Chanakya, "Taxation should not be a painful process for the people. There should be leniency and caution while deciding the tax structure. Ideally, governments should collect taxes like a honeybee, which sucks just the right amount of honey from the flower so that both can survive. Taxes should be collected in small and not in large proportions".

Chanakya, apart from being a man of wisdom and unfailing strategies, propounded the *Nitishastra*, the ideal way of living for every individual. He looked at the country like a person surrounded by problems. He worked at the total annihilation of problems by the roots. The reappearance of troubles only shows its growth. Chanakya's art of diplomacy is well known across India and practiced in the areas of defence, strategy formation and foreign relations.

As a person, Chanakya has been described variously as a saint, ruthless administrator, king maker, a devoted nationalist, selfless ascetic, and a person devoid of all morals. He created controversy by propagating that ends justify the means, and a ruler should use any means to attain his goals and his actions required no moral sanction. The *Arthaśāstra* is unique because of its rational approach and unabashed advocacy of *realpolitik*. His views were dimensionally novel. He recommended espionage and the liberal use of provocative agents as machineries of the state. In politics, he even attested the use of false accusations and killings by a king's secret agent without any ambiguity. The observance of morals and ethics was secondary to the interests of the ruler. Some of his stark views have made him an ambivalent personality for the world. Chānakya is often compared to Machiavelli, Aristotle and Plato, exemplifying his influential status. Chanakya envisioned India as a nation which would place itself as a great power—politically, economically and socially.

Kautilya was no warmonger by temperament. If the end could be achieved by non-military means, by methods of intrigue, duplicity and fraud, he did not advocate an armed conflict: "When the advantages derivable from peace and war are of equal character, one should prefer peace; for disadvantages, of power and wealth, sojourning and sin, are ever attending upon war." He also wrote that: "The arrow shot by an archer may or may not kill a single person; but skilful intrigue devised by wise men, may kill even those who are in the womb". Elsewhere, in a different context he writes that 'Whoever is inferior to another shall make peace; whoever is superior shall wage war."

This brings us to the consideration of another important characteristic of Kautilya's mental make-up, viz., his predilection for fraud and duplicity, in other words, his non-moral attitude. Almost every chapter of the *Arthaśāstra* bears the impress of this Machiavellian outlook. Kautilya apparently believed that the ends justifies the means. He was not scrupulous in the employment of wine, women, poison or spies for achievement of the objective.

He did not admit the intrusion of ethics into a discussion of politics and war. There is, however, one slight difference. In his *Discourses*, Machiavelli suggests that it is only from warfare that he would exclude ethics as irrelevant. In the *Arthaśāstra*, Kautilya makes no such averment; he tacitly warns morality from the threshold.

THE *ARTHAŚĀSTRA* AN OVERVIEW

Till about the dawn of the 20th century there was a misconception in the Western world that everything in ancient India was moved by otherworldly considerations, and that its society was ignorant of statecraft, social affairs and administration. The turning point which removed this misconception was the discovery of Kautilya's *Arthaśāstra* in Sanskrit. Although the Puranas, Panchatantra, Buddhist and Jain scriptures mention the *Arthaśāstra*, there was no written compilation of the work available. The credit for making it accessible must go to the Sanskrit scholar and librarian, Dr. Rudrapatnam Shamasastry. In his preface to the 1915 English translation of Kautilya's *Arthaśāstra*, Shamasastry mentions that an unnamed *pandit* from the Tanjore district handed over a manuscript with a commentary by Bhattasvamin to the Mysore Government Oriental Library. Among the libraries and research institutions in India which preserve rare palm leaf manuscripts, the Mysore Oriental Library (now called the Oriental Research Institute) is well-known.

Even at a young age, Shamasastry showed a remarkable skill in learning the Vedas, the Upanishads and other sacred lore. Before he was forty, he had mastered most of the Vedas, the Vedangas, and classical Sanskrit, German, French and a few more foreign languages. In addition, he had learnt how to decipher several Oriental scripts. Shamasastry was a devoted and sincere librarian and, even though the job of dealing with ancient manuscripts, most of which were in torn condition and quite dusty, was difficult, risky and monotonous, he was dedicated to his job and took pleasure in his work. One day, sometime in 1905, he picked up some palm leaf manuscripts and on keen examination, was pleasantly surprised to discover that it was the *Arthaśāstra* of Kautilya. Examining it from several standpoints, Shamasastry was convinced that it was a genuine work of Kautilya. In his introduction to the book written in 1909, he writes that he was convinced beyond doubt that Kautilya's genuine work was a literary classic of the ancient world. It did not take long for the discovery to get publicity.

Shamasastry translated the work from this manuscript. Later, other manuscripts of the Kautilya *Arthaśāstra* were discovered. Indian scholars such as T. Ganapati Sastri and Indologists from Europe kept adding to its editions and interpretation. An excellent edition for the English-language reader has been done by Professor R.P. Kangle of Bombay University, which was published in three parts between 1961 and1965 as the Kautilya *Arthasastra*. The introduction in the first part of Kangle's book provides the status and location of the various manuscripts of the work.

The history of ancient India pertaining to the 4th century BC, shows that it was Kautilya, also known as Vishnugupta or Chānakya, who overthrew the ruling Nanda dynasty and anointed Chandragupta Maurya as the King. It was this Kautilya who wrote the *Arthaśāstra* which is a monumental treatise on administration and civic affairs. Kautilya was a student of the Taxila (now in Pakistan) University (then called Takshashila), and the very first university to be founded in the world as early as in 700 B.C. He later taught in the same university for about four years. This comprehensive work must have been written sometime between 321–296 BC. It is a practical guide not only on running governmental organisations but is also a work that deals with duties of Kings, Ministers, local officials, methods of diplomacy etc. including ways and means of defeating an enemy. Encyclopaedic in its coverage many scholars have wondered how one head could carry such a vast knowledge.

The *Arthaśāstra* is a single treatise on the Science of Politics which has been prepared mostly by bringing together the pedagogies of ancient teachers for the acquisition and protection of the earth. The aim of the *Arthaśāstra* is thus to teach the ruler how to acquire and protect a kingdom. It is divided into 15 books *(adhikarnas)*, 150 chapters, 180 sections (*prakaranas*) and 6,000 *slokas*. The books are arranged in a manner that the initial books deal with internal administration and the later books on a state's relations with its neighbours. The Kautilya *Arthaśāstra* is a vast volume on statecraft—more than 600 pages in its English translation. Of the fifteen books which the treatise comprises, the first five deal with what is called *tantra,* which is akin to the internal administration of the state. The next eight, deal with *davpa* and they relate to the relationship of the state with the neighbouring states. The last two books contain subjects that are miscellaneous in character.

Book One deals mainly with the training of the prince for the arduous duties of ruling a state. It also discusses the question of appointment of ministers and other officers necessary for the administration of a state. This prepares the ground for the establishment of a benevolent monarchy. It discusses such as the daily routine to be normally followed by the ruler and so on. Kautilya has provided an exhaustive and illustrative description of the duties, responsibilities and role of the king, prince(s), ministers, and other state officials. As for the state's political administration, Kautilya provided a full-fledged commentary as to how this should be effectively undertaken. The contents of the first book include Association with Elders, Control over the Senses, Appointment of Ministers, Appointment of Councillors and Chaplain, Ascertainment of the Integrity or the Absence of Integrity of Ministers by means of Secret Tests, Appointment of Persons in Secret Service, Rules for Secret Servants, Keeping a Watch over the Seducible and Non-seducible Parties in One's Own Territory, Winning over the Seducible and Non-seducible Parties in the Enemy's Territory, The Topic of Counsel, Rules for the Envoy, Guarding against Princes, The Conduct of a Prince in Disfavour, Behaviour towards a Prince in Disfavour, Rules for the

King, Regulations for the Royal Residence, and Concerning the Protection of the King's Own Person.

Book Two principally describes the details of the various executive officers of the state. The opics include: Settlement of the Countryside, Disposal of Non-agricultural Land, Construction of Forts, Lay-out of the Fortified City, The Work of Storekeeping by the Director of Stores, The Setting up of Revenue by the Administrator, The Topic of Accounts in the Records and Audit Office, Recovery of Revenue Misappropriated by State Employees, Inspection of (the work of) Officers, The Topic of Edicts, Examination of the Precious Articles to be Received into the Treasury, The Starting of Mines and Factories, The Superintendent of Gold in the Workshop, The Activity of the Goldsmith in the Market highway, The Superintendent of the Magazine, The Director of Trade, The Director of Forest-produce, The Superintendent of the Armoury, Standardisation of Weights and Measures, Measures of Space and Time, The Collector of Customs and Tolls, The Superintendent of Yarns and Textiles, The Director of Agriculture, The Controller of Spirituous Liquors, The Supervisor of Animal Slaughter, The Superintendent of Courtesans, The Controller of Shipping, The Superintendent of Cattle, The Superintendent of Horses, The Superintendent of Elephants, The Superintendent of Chariots, The Superintendent of Foot-soldiers, The Activity of the Commandant of the Army, The Superintendent of Passports, The Superintendent of Pasture-lands, The Activity of the Administrator, Secret Agents in the Disguise of Householders, Traders and Ascetics, and Rules for the City Superintendent.

Kautilya opines in a most modern way that sovereignty is practicable only with the cooperation of others and all administrative measures are to be taken after proper deliberations. He recommends a strict code of conduct for himself and his administrators.

Kautilya has seriously considered the problem of corruption. He has listed about forty ways of embezzling government funds.

However, he is very practical about the problem and avers that it is as difficult to discover the honesty or otherwise of an officer as it is to find out whether or not it was the fish that drank the water. One of the core themes of this chapter is that the *Arthaśāstra* of equates political governance with economic governance. The end is economic governance while political governance is a means. Good governance is basic to the Kautilyan idea of administration. Good governance and stability are inextricably linked. If rulers are responsive, accountable, removable, recallable, there is stability. If not, there is instability. This is even more relevant in the present democratic set up. Kautilya's precepts may have been in the context of the monarchical set up. However, present rulers and administrators should be endowed with similar qualities.

In stark contrast to the emphasis that the *Arthaśāstra* assigns to rural (village) development, agriculture, and the textile industry, the status quo in India is that these spheres have been neglected. In the sphere of economic administration, India of today has much to learn from Kautilya's *Arthaśāstra*. Kautilya recommends severe penalties on the officials of public enterprises which incurred losses, and rewards for those who showed profits. Profit was essential in Kautilya's scheme of running a country's administration. Some of the ground rules and measures suggested in the *Arthaśāstra*, particularly those which pertain to matters relating to budget, accounts and audit, are applicable to present day India.

Though the kingdom was a feudal monarchy, it had a well structured administrative machinery, containing various departments and the heads of these departments were charged with well specified responsibilities; They were expected to run the team actively, efficiently prudently and profitably; the kingpin of administration was the King himself who was advised by a group of councillors, ministers and other high officials, who were carefully selected by the king himself after careful scrutiny of their character, background and leadership qualities.

Book Three, which is concerned with law and order and its administration, reproduces a complete code of law. This book concerns judges and the subjects include: Determination of Valid and Invalid Transactions, Filing of Lawsuits, Marriage, Partition of Inheritance, Immovable Property, Non-observance of Conventions, Non-payment of Debts, Concerning Deposits, Law concerning Slaves and Labourers, Undertakings in Partnership, Rescission of Sale and Purchase, Non-conveyance of Gifts, Sale without Ownership, The Relation of Ownership, Forcible Seizure, Verbal Injury, Physical Injury, Gambling and Betting, besides miscellaneous issues.

Kautilya distinguished six different kinds of interests: compound interest, periodical interest, stipulated interest, daily interest, and the use of a pledged article. Indeed the idea of expressing interest as a percent originated in India. Thus overall the Kautilyan system of interest seems quite elaborate, complex and even modern. In the *Arthaśāstra*, there is a definite effort to formulate a wage policy based on the realistic understanding of the economic, social and political factors. The emerging policy must be just, and must be consistent with the interest of the state. For Kautilya, the State is a party to any labour or wage legislation together with farmers, merchants and industrialists.

Book Four deals with suppression of crime. It shows how to trace, track and punish thieves, murderers, dacoits, and other criminals. The subjects covered include: Keeping a Watch over Artisans and Traders, Remedial Measures during Calamities, Guarding against Persons with Secret Means of Income, Detection of Criminals through. Secret Agents in the Disguise of Holy Men, Arrest on Suspicion, with the Stolen Article and by Indications of the Act, Inquest on Sudden Deaths, Investigation through Interrogation and through Torture, Keeping a Watch over Officers of All Departments, Redemption from the Cutting of Individual Limbs, The Law of Capital Punishment, Simple and with Torture, Violation of Maidens, and Punishment for Transgression. In Kautilya's state, the king could severely punish corrupt officials, however highly they were placed. In India, those in political office are rarely convicted even if they are corrupt or proved guilty of committing certain offences.

Kautilya identified several areas of State intervention to facilitate the economic life of the country. His idea of the Passport corresponds to the modern version of this document that facilitates movement of people. This is perhaps the first instance of an institutionalised concept of passports to regulate the flow of people across borders. Kautilya said that whoever is provided with a pass shall be at liberty to enter into, or go out of, the country.

Kautilya realised that the role of the State was to ensure that commercial activities do not violate laws or are harmful for the consumer and if the State did not establish and enforce codes of conduct, it would, in fact, raise transaction costs. The lack of trust and guarantee of quality would diminish commerce and increase search and verification costs for agents undertaking commercial transactions. Kautilya explicitly states that adulteration of grains, oils, alkalis, salts, scents, and medicinal articles with similar articles of no quality shall be punished with a fine.

The consumer/buyer is provided safeguards by Kautilya, e.g. the sale or mortgage of articles such as timber, iron, brilliant stones, ropes, skins, earthenware, threads, fibrous garments, and woolen clothes as superior, although they are really inferior, shall be punished with a fine. He states that the Superintendent of Commerce shall fix a profit of five per cent over and above the fixed price of local commodities, and ten per cent on foreign produce. Merchants who enhance the price or realize profit even to the extent of half a *pana* more than the above in the sale or purchase of commodities shall be punished with a fine.

Kautilya recommends that public servants, while engaged in work, they shall be daily examined; for, men are naturally fickle-minded and like horses at work exhibit constant change in their temper. Hence the agency and tools, which they make use of, the place and time of the work they are engaged in, as well as the precise form of the work, the outlay, and the results shall always, be ascertained... hence the chief officer of each department (*adhikarana*) shall thoroughly scrutinize the real amount of the work done, the receipts realised from, and the expenditure incurred in that departmental work both in detail and in the aggregate.

Kautilya admitted that some degree of corruption would always exist, and cannot be scrutinised perfectly. 'It is possible to mark the movements of birds flying high up in the sky; but not so is it possible to ascertain the movement of government servants of hidden purpose. He therefore recommends strictest punishment, both material and corporal, as a disincentive to cheat.

Book Five deals with Secret Conduct and miscellaneous aspects such as measures that may be necessary in emergencies, and steps to be taken against seditious persons. It also lays down scales of salaries for different categories of state servants. It also explains how a candidate for a high office should endeavour to secure and retain it. Finally, it gives advice to chief minister on ensuring continuity of rule on the demise of the ruling monarch. Its contents include: the Infliction of secret Punishment, Replenishment of the Treasury, Concerning the Salaries of State Servants, Proper Conduct for a Dependent and a Courtier, Continuance of the Kingdom and the Sovereignty.

Kautilya considered trade the third pillar of economic activity and in consonance with this the *Arthaśāstra* details every aspect of trade For instance, apart from promoting trade by improving infrastructure, the state was required to keep trade routes free of harassment by courtiers, state officials, thieves, and frontier guards. Kautilya appears to mistrust traders believing them to be thieves, with a propensity to from cartels to fix prices and make excessive profits as also to deal in stolen property. He prescribed heavy fines for discouraging such offences by traders and with a view to consumer protection.

It was also enjoined upon the frontier officers to ensure the safe passage of the merchandise and to make good any loss incurred. Responsibility to recompense loss to traders vested with the village headman barring, of course, goods that were stolen or sent away. Further if any property of trader was lost or driven away in an area between villages, the person responsible was the Chief Superintendent of Pastures. Finally, if the responsibility could not be assigned on any official, the people of the village within whose boundaries the loss had occurred were collectively responsible to the trader.

Book Six deals with the Constituent Elements of a State, Peace and Activity, with the Circle of Kings as the Basis. It enumerates the qualities necessary to make each of the seven *prakratis* or constituents of the state ideal. It also describes *rajamandala* or circle of kings as a preliminary to a discussion on the states' relations with its neighbours.

Book Seven contains elaborate discussion on the way in which each of the six *gunas* on measures of foreign policy may be used in the various situations that are prone to arise, the ultimate goal set before the ruler is conquest of the world. Here various ways in which rivals can be outwitted by stratagems and devises overcome by force have been mentioned. The subjects covered include: Enumeration of the Six Measures of Foreign Policy, Determination of Measures in Decline, Stable Condition and Advancement, Conduct when Seeking Shelter, Adherence to Policies by the Equal, the Weaker and the Stronger King, Peace-treaties by the Weaker King, Staying Quiet after Making War, Staying Quiet after Making Peace, Marching after Making War, Marching after Making Peace, Marching together with other Kings, Considerations regarding an Attack on a Vulnerable King and the Natural Enemy, Causes leading to Decline, Greed and Disaffection, Reflection on Confederated Allies, the March of Two Kings who have entered into a Treaty of Alliance, Treaties with Stipulations, without Stipulations and with Deserters, Peace and War connected with the Dual Policy, Conduct for the King about to be Attacked, The Different Kinds of Allies Fit to be Helped, Pacts for securing an Ally, Money, Land and an Undertaking, Considerations regarding the King Attacking in the Rear, Recoupment of Powers that have become Weak, Reasons for Entrenching Oneself in a Fort after Making War with a Powerful King, Conduct for the King Surrendering with his Troops, Conduct for the King Subjugating other Kings by Force, The Making of Peace, Liberation of a Hostage, Conduct towards the Middle King, Conduct towards the Neutral King, and Conduct towards the Circle of Kings.

Book Eight is concerned with *vyasanas,* that is, calamities, shortcomings or weaknesses affecting the various *prakratis.* It is necessary to overcome the calamity before any aggressive activity can be undertaken. The book details the Group of Calamities of the Constituent Elements, Considerations regarding Calamities of the King and Kingship, The Vices of Man, Afflictions, Hindrances, Stoppages of Payment to the Treasury, Calamities of the Army, and Calamities of the Ally.

Book Nine concerns the activity of the King about to march on a campaign. It deals with preparation for war and describes the kinds of troops that could be mobilised for an expedition, *inter alia,* the proper season for the start of the expedition, the precaution to be taken and inherent dangers to be guarded against, before starting the expedition etc. The contents include: Ascertainment of the Relative Strength or Weakness of Power, Place and Time, Seasons for Marching on an Expedition, Occasions for the Employment of different kinds of Troops, Merits of Equipping different kinds of Troops for War, The Work of employing suitable Troops against Enemy Troops, Consideration of Revolts in the Rear, Counter-measures against Risings of Constituents in the Outer Regions and in the Interior, Consideration of Losses, Expenses and Gains, Dangers from Officers in the Outer Regions and the Interior, Dangers Connected with Traitors and Enemies, Dangers Associated with Advantage, Disadvantage and Uncertainty, and Overcoming These Dangers by the Use of the Different Means.

Book Ten is essentially concerned with fighting and the various methods of warfare. It also describes the battle array and even petty matters relating to camping ground, and such allied topics. The detailed topics are: Setting up of the Camp, March from the Camp,

Guarding Troops during the Calamities of the Army and at the Time of Attack, Various Types of Covert Fighting, Encouraging One's Own Troops, Disposition of One's Troops to Counteract Enemy Troops, Ground Suitable for Fighting, Functions of the Infantry, the Cavalry, the Chariots and the Elephants, Arrangement of Battle-arrays in Wings, Flanks and Front in accordance with the Strength of Troops, Distribution of Strong and Weak Troops, Modes of Fighting of the Infantry, the Cavalry, the Chariots and the Elephants, Arrangement of the Staff, the Snake, the Circle and the Diffuse Arrays, and Arranging Counter arrays against Them.

Book Eleven has only one chapter explaining how the would-be conqueror *(vijigisu)* should subjugate *samghas* or independent oligarchial principalities. It deals with Ways of Resorting to the Policy of sowing Dissensions, and Forms of Secret Punishment.

Book Twelve shows how a weak king, when threatened by a strong king, should frustrate the latter's designs and ultimately overcome him. It deals with; The Mission of the Envoy, Fight with the weapon of Diplomacy, Assassination of the enemy's Army Chiefs, Stirring up the Circle of Kings, Secret Use of Weapons, Fire and Poison, Destruction of the enemy's Supplies, Reinforcements and Foraging Raids, Overreaching the enemy by Trickery and by Force, Victory of the Single King etc.

Book Thirteen is mainly concerned with the conquest of the enemies' fortified capital by subterfuges or fighting. It also describes how the conquered territory should be ruled by the conqueror—the *vijigisu. Its chapters include:* Instigation to Sedition, Drawing Out the enemy by means of Stratagems, Employment of Secret Agents, Laying Siege to a Fort, Storming a Fort, and Pacification of a Conquered Territory.

Book Fourteen describes various secret remedies and occult practices useful for getting rid of enemies or traitors or people prone to indulge in committing or adopting treachery or treason. The topics include: Secret Practices for the Destruction of Enemy Troops, Deceiving by means of Occult Practices, and Counter-measures against Injuries to One's Own Troops.

Finally, **Book Fifteen** describes and illustrates from the text itself the thirty-two *tantrayuktis* or methods of treating a subject.

It is the peculiar characteristic of the *Arthaśāstra* that it went into full details or even minute points connected with its subject matter, and at times it appears prolix or even prosaic. The impression of prolixity that is sometimes created is due to Chanakya's endeavour to speculate, imagine and foresee eve possible eventuality and the related details in any particular situation. It does not show any difference in style, both of versification and prose i.e. *bhasya.* This style of writing is not queer as the tendency in ancient India was to versify the teaching in many branches of learning, particularly if they had a practical use or application. Also versification is useful for memorising. Prose style has been used because it is intended as an abstract of the entire earlier teaching on the subject.

The style of *Arthaśāstra* continuously exhibits a mixture of prose and verse which is common in *sutra* works. Its tenseness is not that of the philosophical or other similar *sutras.* The text, on many occasions, is found difficult, because of the technical nature of its contents and the many technical words used therein. On the whole, it can be claimed that it is easy to understand and grasp the text provided the technical nature of its contents is borne in mind. The *sutras* are simple in construction and free from obscurity caused by long compounds or involved expressions. The *slokas*—stanzas or verses—are characterised by extreme simplicity. It is true that at some places one is not quite sure of the meaning of many words and expressions used in the text. Therefore, the interpretation of many passages in the text has remained uncertain. The vocabulary and language of the *Arthaśāstra* shows striking peculiarities. There are numerous technical terms. Many of them are defined in the *Arthaśāstra* itself, but there are others that are not defined; and they are to be construed either by inference or implication. Nevertheless, after all allowances have been made, it can be maintained that the text is not difficult in style and comprehension.

Kautilya believed in the adage "*Yatha Raja Thatha Prajah*" (As the King is, so will be the people). Therefore he laid down the condition that an ideal King is one who has the highest qualities of leadership, intellect, energy and personal attributes..

The largest sections of the *Arthaśāstra* cover diplomacy and warfare. Kautilya advocates prudence in pursuing the two basic foreign policy aims: Securing the state's security against foreign aggression and expanding the state at the expense of other states. To these ends, diplomacy and intelligence or covert operations are preferable to waging war. Employing guile in statecraft is better than fixating on military force. The ruler and his advisers must carefully calculate the correlation of forces before launching war. Short-term gains through immediate action must be balanced against long-term gains by waiting for the right moment to act.

Kautilya also develops the geometry of foreign policy. The Kautilyan state is surrounded by concentric circles of surrounding states. The states of the first circle are 'natural enemies, because they stand in the way of the state's natural expansionist drive. A second circle of states represents potential allies because their interests are colliding with those of the second circle. The third circle of states consists of potential enemies because they have converging interests with the first circle and conflicting interest with the second. Kautilya anticipates the dictum that the enemy of my enemy is my friend.

The vast conceptional content of the *Arthaśāstra* is not the exclusive creation of just one man—Kautilya. He himself refers to more than 100 source books, which however have all been lost. Thus, Kautilya has synthesised ancient India's accumulated knowledge on statecraft, economics, military strategy, judicial and intelligence matters. Up to the 1990s, there was hardly any interest in Kautilya outside India, but, since then—parallel to the growing international weight of India—the importance of Kautilya has increasingly been realised in the West.

Of course, today's India by no means resembles the Kautilyan state. However, Kautilya has significantly shaped the Indian way of statecraft. If we want to understand India's strategic culture, we should better learn more about Kautilya and his *Arthaśāstra*.

The *Arthaśāstra* has endured the test of time and withstood the test of credibility. When a thinker demonstrates vision and foresight it is useful to understand the elements of this thought that have present applicability. It is a treatise that encapsulates in many ways the complexity of our current world. The problems that existed then persist in a more widespread and magnified manner in the contemporary world.

CONDUCT OF FOREIGN POLICY

The Elements of Sovereignty

The seven elements of sovereignty are:

- The king;
- The minister;
- The country;
- The fort;
- The treasury;
- The army; and
- The ally.

The *Mandala* (Circle of Kings)

A king possessed of good character, and having the best elements of sovereignty, is the fountain of policy. He is termed the *vijigisu* (conqueror). These are the (twelve) primary kings.

- A king ruling contiguous to the conqueror's territory is an enemy.
- A king contiguous to the enemy, but separated from the conqueror only by the enemy, is a ally (of the conqueror).
- A neighbouring foe of considerable power is styled an enemy; and when he is involved in calamities, he becomes assailable; and when he has little or no help, he becomes destructible; he deserves to be harassed or reduced. Such are the aspects of an enemy.

- In front of the conqueror and close to his enemy, would be situated kings such as the conqueror's ally. Next to him, the enemy's ally, and next to the last, the conqueror's ally's ally, and next, the enemy's ally's ally.
- In the rear of the conqueror, there would be situated a rearward enemy (*párshnigráha*), a rearward ally (*ákranda*), an ally of the rearward enemy (*párshnigráhásárá),* and an ally of the rearward ally (*ákrandására).*
- That foe who occupies a territory close to that of the conqueror is a natural enemy; while he who is merely antagonistic and creates enemies for the conqueror is a factitious enemy.
- He whose friendship is derived from father and grandfather, and who is situated close to the territory of the immediate enemy of the conqueror is a natural ally; while he whose friendship is courted for self-maintenance is an acquired ally.
- A king who occupies a territory close to both the conqueror and his immediate enemy in front and who is capable of helping both the kings, whether united or not, or of resisting either of them individually is termed a *Madhyama* (mediatory) king.
- He who is situated beyond the territory of any of the above kings and who is very powerful and capable of helping the enemy, the conqueror, and the *Madhyama* king together or individually, or of resisting any of them individually, is a neutral king (*udásína*).

The conqueror, his ally, and his ally's ally are the three primary kings constituting a circle of states. As each of these three kings possesses the five elements of sovereignty, such as the minister, the country, the fort, the treasury, and the army, a circle of states consists of eighteen elements.

Thus, the (three) Circles of States having the enemy (of the conqueror), the *Madhyama* king, or the neutral king at the centre of each of the three circles, are different from that of the conqueror. Thus there are four primary Circles of States, twelve kings, sixty elements of sovereignty, and seventy-two elements of states. Each of the twelve primary kings have their elements of sovereignty. Strength is power, and happiness is the end.

Strength is of three kinds: power of deliberation is intellectual strength; the possession of a prosperous treasury and a strong army is the strength of sovereignty; and martial power is physical strength.

The end is also of three kinds: that which is attainable by deliberation; that which is attainable by the strength of sovereignty; and that which is to be secured by perseverance.

The possession of power and happiness in a greater degree makes a king superior to another; in a less degree, inferior; and in an equal degree, equal. Hence a king shall always endeavour to augment his own power and elevate his happiness.

A king who is equal to his enemy in the matter of his sovereign elements shall, in virtue of his own righteous conduct or with the help of those who are hostile or conspiring against his enemy, endeavour to defeat his enemy. However, if his enemy, possesses immense power, but in the near future, could hurt the elements of his own sovereignty, the conqueror may allow his enemy to grow in strength and to attain success for the time being.

Conduct of Foreign Policy

Kautilya's desire was for his king to conquer the world. To that end, the ruler should know how to defeat his enemies and rule for the general good. The *Arthaśāstra* is based on political realism. It does not offer how the world should or ought to work, but rather how the world does work and the measures that a king must sometimes take to maintain the common good of the state.

Kautilyan foreign policy offers the theory that an immediate neighbouring state is an enemy and a neighbour's neighbour, separated from oneself by the intervening enemy, is a ally. The conqueror would thus affect the line of allies and enemies, as well as the differing types of allies and enemies a conquering king has. Kautilya describes a Circle of States like a wheel with the conqueror at the hub. His allies are pulled towards him along the spikes although they may be parted by enemy territory. When appropriate, the conquering king shall apply the six methods of foreign policy, known as the six-fold policy, to the various components of his Circle of States. These methods work interdependently and bind others to the conqueror so he may do as he pleases with them when necessary.

The Six-Fold Policy

Kautilya stated that the Circle of States is the source of the six forms of state-policy policy. These are:

1. Peace (*sandhi*)
2. War (*vigraha*)
3. Observance of neutrality (*ásana*)
4. Marching (*yána*)
5. Alliance (*samsraya*)
6. Making peace with one and waging war with another (*dvaidhíbháva*).

Though there are two primary forms of policy, peace and war, Kautilya held that as their conditions differ, there are six forms of policy. He explained that:

- Agreement with pledges is peace;
- An offensive operation is war;
- Indifference is neutrality;
- Making preparations is marching;
- Seeking the protection of another is alliance; and
- Making peace with one and waging war with another is a dual policy.

Kautilya further explained that:

- Whoever is inferior to another shall make peace with him;

- Whoever is superior in power shall wage war;
- Whoever thinks no enemy can hurt me, nor am I strong enough to destroy my enemy, shall observe neutrality;
- Whoever is possessed of necessary means shall march against his enemy;
- Whoever is devoid of necessary strength to defend himself shall seek the protection of another;
- Whoever thinks that help is necessary to work out an end shall make peace with one and wage war with another.

A wise ruler should observe that form of policy which, in his opinion, enables him to work for the progress of his state, and at the same time to harass similar aims of his enemy. Thus, a ruler who thinks that he is growing in power more rapidly, both in quality and quantity (than his enemy), may neglect his enemy's progress for the time-being. If any two kings hostile to each other find the progress of their respective works to be equal, they shall make peace with each other. No king shall follow that form of policy, which causes him loss of profit from his own ventures, but which entails no such loss on the enemy.

The Nature of Alliances

When the advantages derivable from peace and war are of equal character, one should prefer peace; for disadvantages, such as the loss of power and wealth are ever-attending upon war. The same holds good in the case of neutrality and war. Of the two forms of policy, (dual policy and alliance), the dual policy is preferable; for whoever adopts it enriches himself, being ever attentive to his own ventures, whereas an allied king has to help his ally at his own expense.

An alliance should be with a king who is stronger than one's neighbouring enemy. In the absence of such a king, one should ingratiate oneself with one's neighbouring enemy, either by supplying money or army or by ceding a part of one's territory and by keeping oneself aloof; for there can be no greater evil to kings than alliance with a king of considerable power, unless one is actually attacked by one's enemy.

A powerless king should behave as a conquered king (towards his immediate enemy); but when he finds that the time of his own ascendancy is at hand he may eliminate the enemy when opportunity affords itself.

A king who is situated between two powerful kings should seek protection from the stronger of the two; or from one of them on whom he can rely. Other options are:

- Make peace with both of them on equal terms. Then he may begin to set one of them against the other and thus cause dissension between them.
- Take the protection of any two immediate kings of considerable power to defend himself against an immediate enemy.
- Having made an alliance with a ruler in a stronghold, he may adopt a dual policy i.e. make peace with one of the two kings, and wage war with the other.
- Adapt to circumstances and make allies with traitors, enemies, and others who are conspiring against both the kings.
- Having made allies with both, he may form a circle of states.
- Make an alliance with the *madhyama* or the neutral king; and with his help put down one of them or both.

The Character of Equal, Inferior and Superior Kings Forms of Agreement made by an Inferior King

A King desirous of expanding his own power shall make use of the six-fold policy. Agreements of peace shall be made with equal and superior kings; and an inferior king shall be attacked. Whoever goes to war with a superior king will be reduced to the same condition as that of a foot-soldier opposing an elephant. It is destructive. War with an equal king brings ruin to both.

- Like a stone striking an earthen pot, a superior king gains decisive victory over an inferior king.
- If a superior king discards the proposal of an inferior king for peace, the latter should take the attitude of a conquered king, or play the part of an inferior king towards a superior.
- When a king of equal power does not like peace, then the same amount of vexation as his opponent has received at his hands should be given to him in return; for it is power that brings about peace between any two kings. A piece of iron that is not made red-hot will combine with another piece of iron.
- When an inferior king is all submissive, peace should be made with him; for when provoked by causing him troubles it will anger him like a wild fire and force him to attack his enemy; and the inferior king will also be favoured by (his) Circle of States.
- When a king in peace with another finds that the impoverished and oppressed subjects of his ally, immigrate into his own territory, then he should, though of inferior power, proclaim war against his ally.
- When one of the two kings at war with each other and equally involved in trouble finds his own troubles to be greater than his enemy's, and thinks that by getting rid of his own trouble his enemy can successful wage war with him, then he should, though possessing greater resources, sue for peace.
- When, either in peace or war, a king finds neither loss to his enemy, nor gain to himself, he should, though superior, observe neutrality.
- When a king finds the troubles of his enemy irremediable, he should, though of inferior power, march against the enemy.

- When a king finds himself threatened by imminent dangers or troubles, he should, though superior, seek the protection of another.
- When a king is sure to achieve his desired ends by making peace with one and waging war with another, he should, though superior, adopt the dual policy.

Neutrality after Proclaiming War or After Concluding a Treaty of Peace

Marching After Proclaiming War or After Making Peace

The March of Combined Powers

Sthána (keeping quiet), *ásana* (withdrawal from hostility), and *upekshana* (negligence) are synonymous with the word *ásana* i.e. neutrality.

When two kings who, though bent on making conquests, are desirous of peace but are unable to proceed against the other, they may keep quiet after proclaiming war or after making peace.

When a king finds it possible to put down by means of his own army, or with the help of an ally, another king of equal or superior power, then having set up proper defences against both internal and external enemies, he may keep quiet after proclaiming war.

The impoverishment of the enemy who is free from troubles must be aimed at (when a king keeps quiet after proclaiming war). As soon as such a king acquires sufficient strength, he will undertake to destroy the enemy. To such a king, the enemy's enemy will send help. Hence, whoever is provided with necessary strength may keep quiet after proclaiming war.

When the policy of keeping quiet after proclaiming war is found to yield unfavourable results, then one shall keep quiet after making peace.

A ruler who has grown in strength, in consequence of keeping quiet after proclaiming war, should proceed to attack his enemy. When a king is so fortunate as to have a powerful ally in front and a powerful ally (*ákranda*) in the rear, both with brave and loyal subjects, while the reverse is the case with his enemies both in front and in the rear, and when he finds it possible for his ally to hold his frontal enemy in check, and for his rear-ally to keep his rear-enemy (*párshnigráha*) at bay, then he may march after proclaiming war against his frontal enemy.

When a king finds himself unable to confront his enemy single-handed and when it is necessary that he should march, then he should make the expedition in combination with kings of inferior, equal, or superior powers.

Considerations on Marching Against an Assailable Enemy and a Strong Enemy

Considerations about the Combination of Powers

The *vijigisu* should march against the strong enemy with fewer troubles, for the troubles of the strong enemy will be augmented when attacked. True, that the worse troubles of the assailable enemy will be still worse when attacked. But when left to himself, the strong enemy under less trouble will endeavour to get rid of his troubles and unite with the assailable enemy or with another enemy in the rear of the conqueror.

When an enemy of virtuous character and under worse troubles is attacked, his subjects will help him; whereas, the subjects of the other of vicious character and under less trouble will be indifferent. Disloyal or indifferent subjects will endeavour to destroy even a strong king. Hence the conqueror should march against that enemy whose subjects are disloyal or oppressed.

A strong enemy of wicked character should be marched against, for when he is attacked, his subjects will not help him, but rather put him down or go to the side of the conqueror. But when the enemy of virtuous character is attacked, his subjects will help him or die with him. Hence, no king should give room to such causes as would bring about impoverishment, greed or disaffection among his people. If, however, they appear, he should at once take remedial measures against them.

Having well considered the causes which bring about peace or war, one should combine with kings of considerable power and righteous character and march against one's enemy.

It is better to march with two kings of lesser power; for the conqueror can depute them to carry out any two different tasks and keep them under his control. When the desired end is achieved, the inferior king will quietly retire after the satisfaction of his superior.

The March of Combined Powers Agreement of Peace With or Without Definite Terms Peace with Renegades

The conqueror should over-reach the enemy close to his territory. He should engage his neighbouring enemy to undertake a simultaneous march with him. If the booty is to be equally divided, it is an agreement of peace; if otherwise, it is overpowering the enemy. An agreement of peace may be made with a promise to carry out a definite task (*paripanita*) or with no such promise (*aparipanita*).

When the conqueror thinks that my enemy (now an ally) has to march through an unknown country, and in difficult terrain then he should make an agreement to carry out a task in a defined area. Then, having kept a neighbouring enemy engaged with another neighbouring enemy, a wise king should proceed against a third king, and having conquered that enemy of equal power, take possession of his territory.

The forms of peace are:

- Peace with no specific end (*akritachikírshá*) i.e. when, by making use of conciliation and other stratagems, an agreement of peace is made and the rights of equal, inferior, and superior powers concerned in the agreement are defined according to their respective positions with no specific end (other than self-preservation).

- Peace with binding terms (*kritasleshana*) i.e. when, by the employment of allies (at the Courts of each other), an agreement of peace is kept secure and the terms observed and strictly maintained so that no dissension may creep among the parties.
- The breaking of peace (*kritavidúshana*) i.e. when, having proved through traitors and spies the treachery of a king, who has made an agreement of peace, the agreement is broken.
- Restoration of peace broken (*apasírnakriyá*) i.e. when reconciliation is made with a servant, or a ally, or any other renegade.

The three forms of battle are: open battle, treacherous battle, and silent battle (i.e. killing an enemy by employing spies when there is no talk of battle at all).

There are four kinds of renegades:

- One who had reason to run away and to return. He can be reconciled with.
- One who had no reason either to run away or to return. He is a fickle-minded person having no explanation to account for his conduct. He should have no terms of reconciliation.
- One who had reason to run away, but none to return. His case is to be well considered (before he is taken back).
- One who had no reason to run away, but had reason to come back. His reasons should be examined; and if he is found to be actuated with good motives, he is to be taken back respectfully; otherwise, he should be kept at a distance.

When a king thinks that "this renegade supplies me with full information about my enemy's weakness, and, therefore, he deserves to remain here; his own people with me are in friendship with my allies and at enmity with my enemies", he may treat such a renegade as deserved. Whoever is injurious to the king's interests should be abandoned, while he who is injurious to the interests of the enemy should be reconciled; and whoever is injurious to the interests of both the king and his enemy should be carefully examined.

Peace and War by Adopting the Dual Policy

Having combined with a neighbouring king, the conqueror may march against another neighbouring king. If he thinks that my enemy will neither capture my rear nor make an alliance with my assailable enemy against whom I am going to march; else he shall have to fight against great odds; then the conqueror may proclaim war against one and make peace with another.

When kings of superior, equal or inferior power make peace with the conqueror and agree to pay a greater, or equal, or less amount of profit in proportion to the army supplied, it is termed an even peace; when it is of the reverse character it is styled uneven peace; and when the profit is proportionally very high, it is termed deception (*atisandhi*).

When a king of inferior power has to make a short march in order to capture an enemy without waging war or to receive some expected profit, he may request a third king of superior power involved under various troubles and misfortunes for the help of the latter's army in return for the payment of a share in the profit less than the strength of the army supplied deserves. If the king to whom this proposal is made is powerful enough to retaliate, he may declare war; but otherwise he may accept the proposal.

When a king proposes peace to another king of equal power on the condition of receiving the help of the latter's army which is strong enough to oppose an enemy's army in return for a payment of a share in the profit proportionally equal to the strength of the army supplied, the latter may accept the terms if the proposer is of good intentions; otherwise he may declare war.

When a king of equal power, capable of receiving the help of an army from another quarter, requests another king in troubles, the help of the latter's army in return for the payment of a share in profit less than the strength of the army supplied deserves, the latter, if powerful, may declare war or otherwise accept the terms.

When a king who is under troubles, who has his works at the mercy of his neighbouring kings, and who has yet to organize an army, requests another king of equal power the help of the latter's army in return for the payment of a share in the profit greater than the strength of the army supplied deserves, the latter may accept the terms if the proposer is of good intentions: otherwise war may be declared.

When, with the desire of putting down a king in troubles due to the diminished strength of the elements of sovereignty, or with the desire of destroying his well-begun work of immense and unfailing profit, or with the intention of striking him in his own place or on the occasion of marching, one, though getting immense subsidy from an assailable enemy of equal, inferior, or superior power, sends demands to him again and again, then he may comply with the demands of the former if he is desirous of maintaining his own power by destroying with the army of the former an impregnable fortress of an enemy or ally of that enemy or laying waste the wild tracts of that enemy, or if he is desirous of exposing the army of the ally to wear and tear even in good roads and good seasons, or if he is desirous of strengthening his own army with that of his ally and, thereby doing down the ally, or winning over the army of the ally.

When a king is desirous of keeping under his power another king of superior or inferior power as an assailable enemy and of destroying the latter after routing another enemy with the help of the latter, or when he is desirous of getting back whatever he has paid (as subsidy), he may send a proposal of peace on the condition of paying more than the cost of the army supplied. If the king to whom this proposal is made is powerful enough to retaliate he may declare war; otherwise he may accept the terms; or he may keep quiet allied with the assailable enemy; or he may supply the proposer of peace with his army full of traitors.

When a king of superior power falls into troubles owing to the weakness of the elements of his sovereignty, and requests of an inferior king the help of the latter's army in return for the payment of a share in the profit proportionally equal to the strength of the army supplied, the latter, if powerful enough to retaliate, may declare war and if otherwise, accept the terms.

The Attitude of an Assailable Enemy; and Allies that Deserve Help

When an assailable enemy who is in danger of being attacked is desirous of taking upon himself the condition which led one king to combine with another against him, or of splitting them from each other, he may propose peace to one of the kings on the condition of paying twice the amount of profit accruing from the combination. The agreement having been made, he may describe to that king the loss of men and money, the hardships of sojourning abroad, the commission of sinful deeds, and the misery and other personal troubles to which that king would have been subjected. When the king is convinced of the truth, the amount promised may be paid; or having made that king incur enmity with other kings, the agreement itself may be broken.

When a king is inclined to cause to another, loss of men and money in the ill-considered undertakings of the latter or to frustrate the latter in the attempt of achieving large profits from well-begun undertakings; or when he means to strike another at their place or while marching; or when he intends to exact subsidy again in combination with the latter's assailable enemy; or when he is in need of money and does not trust to his ally, he may be satisfied with a small profit.

When a king has in view the necessity of helping a ally or of destroying an enemy, or the possibility of acquiring much wealth (in return for his help) or when he intends to utilize in future the services of the one now obliged by him, he may reject the offer of large profit at the present in preference of a small gain in future.

When a king means to help another from the clutches of traitors or enemies or of a superior king threatening the very existence of the latter, and intends thereby to set an example of rendering similar help to himself in future, he should receive no profit either at the present or in the future.

When a king means to harass the people of an enemy or to break the agreement of peace between a ally and a foe, or when he suspects another's attack upon himself, and when owing to any of these causes, he wants to break peace with his ally, he may demand from the latter an enhanced amount of profit long before it is due. The latter under these circumstances may demand a procedure (*krama*) either at the present or in the future.

Whoever of the two, the conqueror or his enemy, who may happen to have a ally in the same *Madhyama* king, helps a *Madhyama* king of true or truer friendship overreaches the other; for, by helping a true ally, he enriches himself, while the other incurs loss of men and money and the difficulties of sojourning abroad. When a *Madhyama* king thus helped is devoid of good qualities, then the enemy overreaches the conqueror: for, such a *Madhyama* king, spending his energies on useless undertakings and receiving help with no idea of returning it, withdraws himself away. The same thing holds good with a neutral king under similar circumstances.

Agreement for the Acquisition of an Ally or Gold

Of the three gains, the acquisition of a ally, of gold, and of territory, accruing from the march of combined powers, territory is the best. Allies and gold can be acquired by means of territory; whereas of a ally and gold, each can be a means to acquire the other.

An agreement under the condition, "let us acquire a ally" is termed even peace; when one acquires a ally and the other makes an enemy, etc., it is termed uneven peace; and when one gains more than the other, it is deception. In an even peace (i.e., agreement on equal terms) whoever acquires a ally of good character or relieves an old ally from troubles, overreaches the other; for help given in misfortune renders friendship very firm.

A temporary ally of submissive nature is better; for such a ally will be a true ally so long as he is helpful; for the real characteristic of friendship lies in giving help. A long-standing ally of limited prospects is better, as a temporary ally of large prospects is likely to withdraw his friendship on account of material loss in the shape of help given, or is likely to expect similar kind of help in return; but a long-standing ally of limited prospects can, in virtue of his long-standing nature, render immense service in the long run.

A small ally easy to be roused is better, for he will not, in his ready preparations, be behind the opportune moment of work, and by virtue of his weakness in power, can be used in any way the conqueror may like; but not so the other of vast territorial power.

Agreement of Peace for the Acquisition of Land

In an agreement of peace for the acquisition of land, of the two kings thus entering into an agreement whoever acquires a rich and fertile land with standing crops overreaches the other. In case of the acquisition of rich land being equal, whoever acquires such land by putting down a powerful enemy overreaches the other; for not only does he acquire territory, but also destroys an enemy and thereby augments his own power. True, there is beauty in acquiring land by putting down a weak enemy; but the land acquired will also be poor, and the king in the neighbourhood who has hitherto been a ally, will now become an enemy.

The enemies being equally strong, he who acquires territory after beating a fortified enemy overreaches the other; for the capture of a fort is conducive to the protection of territory. Land which is close to a powerless enemy is easily maintained while that bordering upon the territory of a powerful enemy has to be kept at the expense of men and money.

A rich land creates many enemies, and the constant enemy will ever be an enemy, whether or not he is helped (with men and money to conciliate him); but a temporary enemy will be quiet either from fear or favour.

Which is better, a small piece of land, not far, or an extensive piece of land, very far? A small piece of land, not far, is better, inasmuch as it can be easily acquired, protected, and defended, whereas the other is of a reverse nature.

Of the above two kinds of land, which is better, that which can be maintained by itself, or that which requires external armed force to maintain? The former is better, as it can be maintained with the army and money produced by itself, whereas the latter is of a reverse character as a military station.

Which is better, acquisition of land from a stupid or a wise king? That acquired from a stupid king is better, as it can be easily acquired and secured, and cannot be taken back, whereas that obtained from a wise king, beloved of his subjects, is of a reverse nature.

Of two enemies, of whom one can only be harassed and another is reducible, acquisition of land from the latter is better; for when the latter is attacked, he, having little or no help, begins to run away, taking his army and treasure with him, and he is deserted by his subjects; whereas the former does not do so, as he has the help of his forts and allies. Of two fortified kings, one who has his forts on a plain is more easily reduced than the other owning a fort in the centre of a river; for a fort in a plain can be easily assailed, destroyed or captured along with the enemy in it, whereas a fort, surrounded by a river requires twice as much effort to capture and supplies the enemy with water and other necessaries of life.

Of two kings, one owning a fort surrounded by a river, and

another having mountainous fortifications, seizing the former's land is better, for a fort in the centre of a river can be assailed by a bridge formed of elephants made to stand in a row in the river or by wooden bridges, or by means of boats; and the river will not always be deep and can be emptied of its water, whereas a fort on a mountain is of a self-defensive nature, and not easy to besiege or to ascend; and when one portion of the army defending it is routed out, the other portions can escape unhurt.

Which is easier, seizing land from those who fight on plains, or from those who fight from low grounds? Seizing the land from the latter is easier, inasmuch as they have to fight in time and space of adverse nature whereas the former can fight anywhere and at any time.

Interminable Agreement

An agreement to colonize waste land is an interminable agreement. Whoever of the two parties of the agreement colonizes a fertile land, reaping the harvest earlier, overreaches the other. A limited tract of land with water is far better than a vast plain, inasmuch as the former is conducive to the growth of crops and fruits throughout the year.

Of two tracts of land, one rich in grains and another in mines, the latter helps the treasury, while the former can fill both the treasury and the store-house; and besides this, the construction of forts and other buildings requires grains. Still, the land containing mines and which yields precious metals to purchase large tracts of land is far better.

Land with a scattered people is better inasmuch as it can be kept under control and is not susceptible to the intrigues of enemies. In colonising a land with four castes, colonisation with the lowest caste is better, inasmuch as it is serviceable in various ways, plentiful, and permanent.

Of cultivated and uncultivated tracts, the uncultivated tract may be suitable for various kinds of agricultural operations; and when it is fertile, adapted for pasture grounds, manufacture of merchandise, mercantile transactions of borrowing and lending, and attractive to rich merchants, it is still far better (than a cultivated tract).

A king who is desirous of getting back land sold for colonisation to another when the latter has lost his men and money in colonising it, should first make an agreement with such a purchaser as is weak, base-born, devoid of energy, helpless, of unrighteous character, addicted to evil ways, trusting to fate, and indiscreet in his actions. An indiscreet colonizer may sometimes betray the weak points of his employer (the conqueror). But, just as he betrays the weak points, so also does he facilitate his destruction by the conqueror.

When a king of immense power compels another to sell a portion of the latter's fertile territory, then the latter may make an agreement with the former and sell the land. This is what is termed unconcealed peace (*anibhritasandhih*).

Agreement for Undertaking a Task

Whoever of the two kings builds an impregnable fortress on a spot naturally best fitted for the purpose with less labour and expenditure overreaches the other. Of forts such as a fort on a plain, in the centre of a river, and on a mountain, that which is mentioned later is of more advantage.

Of irrigational works (*setu-bandha*), that area which is of perennial water is better than that which is fed with water drawn from other sources; and of works containing perennial water, that which can irrigate an extensive area is better.

Of timber forests, whoever plants a forest which produces valuable articles, which expands into wild tracts, and which possesses a river on its border overreaches the other, for a forest containing a river is self-dependent and can afford shelter in calamities.

Of mines, whoever exploits with less labour and expenditure a mine of valuable output and of easy communication overreaches the other.

Considerations about an Enemy in the Rear

When the conqueror and his enemy simultaneously proceeded to capture the rear of their respective enemies who are engaged in an attack against others, he who captures the rear of one who is possessed of vast resources gains more advantages (*atisandhatte*); for one who is possessed of vast resources has to put down the rear-enemy only after doing away with one's frontal enemy already attacked, but not one who is poor in resources and who has not realised the desired profits.

Resources being equal, he who captures the rear of one who has made vast preparations gains more advantages for one who has made vast preparations has to put down the enemy in the rear only after destroying the frontal enemy, but not one whose preparations are made on a small scale and whose movements are, therefore, obstructed by the Circle of States.

Preparations being equal, he who captures the rear of one who has marched out with all the resources gains more advantages; for one whose base is undefended is easy to be subdued, but not one who has marched out with a part of the army after having made arrangements to defend the rear.

Troops taken being of equal strength, he who captures the rear of one who has gone against a wandering enemy gains more advantages; for one who has marched out against a wandering enemy has to put down the rear-enemy only after obtaining an easy victory over the wandering enemy; but not one who has marched out against an entrenched enemy, for one who has marched out against an entrenched enemy will be repelled in his attack against the enemy's forts and will, after his return, find himself between the rear-enemy, and the frontal enemy who is possessed of strong forts.

Of attacks from the rear and front, that which affords opportunities of carrying on a treacherous fight (*mantrayuddha*) is preferable. Even at considerable loss of men and money, the destruction of an enemy is desirable.

Loss of men and money being equal, he who entirely destroys first his frontal enemy, and next attacks his rear-enemy gains more advantages; when both the conqueror and his enemy are severally engaged in destroying their respective frontal enemies, he who destroys a frontal enemy of deep rooted enmity and of vast resources, gains more advantages.

Recovery of Lost Power

When the conqueror is attacked by the combined army of his enemies, he may tell their leader: "I shall make peace with you; this is the gold, and if I become your ally; your gain is doubled; it is not worthy of you to augment at your own expense the power of your enemies who keep a friendly appearance now; for gaining in power, they will put you down in the long run."

Or he may tell the leader so as to break their combination: "Just as an innocent person like me is now attacked by the combined army of these kings, so the very same kings in combination will attack you at an opportune time; for power intoxicates the mind; hence break their combination."

The combination being broken, he may set the leader against the weak among his enemies; or offering inducements, he may set the combined power of the weak against the leader; or in whatever way be may find it to be conducive to his own prosperity, in that way he may make the leader incur the displeasure of others, and thus frustrate their attempts; or showing the prospect of a larger profit, he may through intrigue, make peace with their leader.

In the absence of a leader, the conqueror may win him over who is the inciter of the combination; or who is of a resolute mind, or who has endeared himself to his people, or who, from greed or fear, joined the combination, or who is afraid of the conqueror, or whose friendship with the conqueror is based upon some consanguinity of royalty, or who is a ally, or who is a wandering enemy,—in the order of enumeration.

He who is in troubles and is apprehensive of an attack from his enemy, should, on the condition of supplying the enemy with army and money, make peace with the enemy on definite terms with reference to place, time, and work; he should also set right any offence he might have given by the violation of a treaty; if he has no supporters, he should find them among his relatives and allies; or he may build an impregnable fortress, for he who is defended by forts and allies will be respected both by his own and his enemy's people.

He who is devoid of a good treasury and army should direct his attention towards the strengthening of the safety and security of the elements of his sovereignty; for the country is the source of all those works which are conducive to treasury and army; the haven of the king and of his army is a strong fort.

He should also adopt the policy of a weak king towards powerful king in view of averting danger from enemies or allies. Thus with the aid of one's own party, the power of deliberation, the treasury, and the army, one should get rid of the clutches of one's enemies.

Measures Conducive to Peace with a Strong and Provoked Enemy

The Attitude of a Conquered Enemy

When a weak king is attacked by a powerful enemy, the former should seek the protection of one who is superior to his enemy and whom his enemy's power of deliberation for intrigue cannot affect. Of kings who are equal in the power of deliberation, difference should be sought in unchangeable prosperity and in association with the aged.

In the absence of a superior king, he should combine with a number of his equals who are equal in power to his enemy and whom his enemy's power of purse, army, and intrigue cannot reach. Of kings who are equally possessed of the power of purse, army, and intrigue, difference should be sought in their capacity for making vast preparations.

In the absence of equals, he should combine with a number of inferior kings who are pure and enthusiastic, who can oppose the enemy, and whom his enemy's power of purse, army, and intrigue cannot react. Of kings who are equally possessed of enthusiasm and capacity for action, a difference should be sought in the opportunity of securing favourable battlefields.

In the absence of any such help, he should seek shelter inside a fort in which his enemy with a large army can offer no obstruction to the supply of food-stuff, grass, firewood and water, but would sustain a heavy loss of men and money. When there are many forts, difference should be sought in their affording facility for the collection of stores and supplies. One should entrench oneself in a fort inhabited by men and provided with stores and supplies.

In the absence of such circumstances, or when the enemy's army is very strong, one may run away abandoning one's fort. Thereafter, having observed the conditions conducive to peace between himself and his enemy, he may make peace; in the absence of such conditions, he may, by taking recourse to threats secure peace or an ally.

Having secured his enemy's protection, he should be like a servant to his master by serving the protector's occasional needs. Any activity should be undertaken only with the permission of his protector. He should also help his protector as much as he can.

The Attitude of a Conquered King

To cause financial trouble to his protector, a powerful vassal king, desirous of making conquests, may, under the permission of his protector, march on countries where the formation of the ground and the climate are favourable for the manoeuvre of his army, his enemy having neither forts, nor any other defensive works, and the conqueror himself having no enemies in the rear.

By means of conciliation and gifts, he should subdue weak kings; and by means of sowing the seeds of dissension and by threats, strong kings. By adopting particular, alternative, or all strategic means, he should subdue his immediate and distant enemies.

By instigating any neighbouring king, he should sow the seeds of dissension. By capturing the enemy in an open battle, or in a treacherous fight, or through a conspiracy, or in the tumult of seizing the enemy's fort by strategic means, he should punish the enemy.

(The king who is desirous of making conquests) should continue in following the same policy towards him, who, among the above kings, is most helpful and keeps the same attitude; should by secret means bring him round who is opposed; should favour the helpful with facilities for giving further help, besides bestowing rewards and honour at all costs upon him; should give relief to him who is under troubles; should receive visitors at their own choice and afford satisfaction to them; should avoid using contemptuous, threatening, defamatory, or harsh words towards them; should like a father protect those who are promised security from fear; should punish the guilty after publishing their guilt; and in order to avoid causing suspicion to the protector, the vassal-king should adopt the procedure of inflicting secret punishments upon offenders.

He should never covet the land, things, and sons and wives of the king slain by him; he should reinstate in their own estates the relatives of the kings slain. He should install in the kingdom the heir-apparent of the king who has died while working (with the conqueror); all conquered kings will, if thus treated, loyally follow the sons and grandsons of the conqueror.

Making Peace and Breaking It

The words *sama* (quiet), *sandhi* (agreement of peace), and *samádhi* (reconcilement), are synonymous. That which is conducive to mutual faith among kings is termed *sama*, *sandhi*, or *samádhi*. Peace, dependent upon honesty or oath is immutable both in this and the next world. It is for this world only that a security or hostage is required for strengthening an agreement.

In case of any apprehension of breach of honesty, whoever takes as security a person capable of controlling the enemy gains more advantages, while he who acts to the contrary is deceived.

In peace made with children as hostages, and in the case of giving a princess or a prince as an hostage, whoever gives a princess gains advantages; for a princess, when taken as an hostage, causes troubles to the receiver, while a prince is of reverse nature.

With regard to two sons, whoever hands over a highborn, brave and wise son, trained in military art, or an only son is deceived, while he who acts otherwise gains advantages. It is better to give a base-born son as an hostage than a high-born one, inasmuch as the former has neither heir-ship nor the right to beget heirs; it is better to give a stupid son than a wise one, inasmuch as the former is destitute of the power of deliberation; better to give a timid son than a brave one, inasmuch as the former is destitute of martial spirit; better, a son who is not trained in military art than one who is trained, inasmuch as the former is devoid of the capacity for striking an enemy; and better one of many sons than an only son, since many sons are not wanted.

Whoever is Rising in Power may Break an Agreement of Peace

The Conduct of a *Madhyama* King, a Neutral King, and of a Circle of States

The third and the fifth states from a *madhyama* king are states friendly to him; while the second, the fourth, and the sixth are unfriendly. If the *madhyama* king shows favour to both of these states, the conqueror should be friendly with him; if he does not favour them, the conqueror should be allyly with those states.

If the *madhyama* king is desirous of securing the friendship of the conqueror's would-be ally, then having set his own and his ally's allies against the *madhyama*, and having separated the *madhyama* from the latter's allies, the conqueror should preserve his own ally; or the conqueror may incite the Circle of States against the *madhyama* by telling them; "this *madhyama* king has grown haughty, and is aiming at our destruction: let us therefore combine and interrupt his march."

If the Circle of States is favourable to his cause, then he may aggrandise himself by putting down the *madhyama*; if not favourable, then having helped his ally with men and money, he should, by means of conciliation and gifts, win over either the leader or a neighbouring king among the kings who hate the *madhyama*, or who have been living with mutual support, or who will follow the one that is won over (by the conqueror), or who do not rise owing to mutual suspicion; thus by winning over a second (king), he should double his own power; by securing a third, he should treble his own power; thus gaining in strength, he should put down the *madhyama* king.

When place and time are found unsuitable for success in the above attempt, he should, by peace, seek the friendship of one of the enemies of the *madhyama* king, or cause some traitors to combine against the *madhyama*; if the *madhyama* king is desirous of reducing the conqueror's ally, the conqueror should prevent it, and tell the ally: "I shall protect you as long as you are weak."

If, among the conqueror's allies who are either reducible or assailable enemies of the *madhyama* king, some undertake to help the *madhyama*, then the conqueror should make peace with a third king; and if among the *madhyama* king's allies who are either reducible or assailable enemies of the conqueror, some are capable of offence and defence and become allyly to the conqueror, then he should make peace with them; thus the conqueror cannot only attain his own ends, but also please the *madhyama* king.

If the *madhyama* king is desirous of securing a would-be ally of the conqueror as a ally, then the conqueror may make peace with another king, or prevent the ally from going to the madhyama, telling him: "It is unworthy of you to forsake a ally who is desirous of your friendship," or the conqueror may keep quiet, if the conqueror thinks that the Circle of States would be enraged against the ally for deserting his own party. If the *madhyama* king is desirous of securing the conqueror's enemy as his ally, then the conqueror should indirectly *(i.e.,* without being known to the *madhyama)* help the enemy with wealth and army.

If the *madhyama* king desires to win the neutral king, the conqueror should sow the seeds of dissension between them. Whoever of the *madhyama* and the neutral kings is esteemed by the Circle of States, his protection should the conqueror seek.

The conduct of the *madhyama* king explains that of the neutral king. If the neutral king is desirous of combining with the *madhyama* king, then the conqueror should so attempt as to frustrate the desire of the neutral king to overreach an enemy or to help a ally or to secure the services of the army of another neutral king. Having thus strengthened himself, the conqueror should reduce his enemies and help his allies, though their position is inimical towards him.

Those who may be inimical to the conqueror are a king who is of wicked character and who is therefore always harmful, a rear-enemy in combination with a frontal enemy, a reducible enemy under troubles, and one who is watching the troubles of the conqueror to invade him.

Those who may be allied with the conqueror are one who marches with him with the same end in view, one who marches with him with a different end in view, one who wants to combine with the conqueror to march (against a common enemy), one who marches under an agreement for peace, one who marches with a set purpose of, his own, one who rises along with others, one who is ready to purchase or to sell either the army or the treasury, and one who adopts the double policy (i.e., making peace with one and waging war with another).

DEFENCE OF A KINGDOM

Setting up a Fort or Camp

On a site declared to be the best according to the science of buildings, the leader (*náyaka*), the carpenter (*vardhaki*), and the astrologer (*mauhúrtika*) should measure a circular, rectangular, or square spot for the camp which should, in accordance with the available space, consist of four gates, six roads, and nine divisions.

Provided with ditches, parapets, walls, doors, and watch towers for defence, the quarters of the king, 1,000 bows long and half as broad, should be situated in one of the nine divisions to the north from the centre, while to the west of it his harem, and at its extremity the army of the harem are to be situated. In his front, the temples; to his right the departments of finance and accounts; and to his left the quarters of elephants and horses mounted by the king himself.

Outside this and at a distance of 100 bows from each other, there should be fixed four cart-poles (*sakatamedhi*) pillars and walls. In the first (of these four divisions), the prime minister and the priest should have their quarters; to its right the store-house and the kitchen: to its left the store of raw products and weapons; in the second division the quarters of the army and of horses and chariots: outside this, hunters and keepers of dogs with their trumpets; also spies and sentinels. To prevent an enemy attack, wells, mounds and thorns should be arranged. The eighteen divisions of sentinels employed for securing the safety of the king should change their timings for watch in turn. In order to ascertain the movements of spies, a timetable of business should also be prepared. Disputes, drinking, social gatherings, and gambling should be prohibited. The system of passports should also be observed. The officer in charge of the boundary (of the camp) should supervise the conduct of the commander-in-chief and the observance of the instructions given to the army.

March of the Camp

Protection of the Army in Times of Distress and Attack

Having prepared a list of the villages and forests situated on the route with reference to their capacity to supply grass, firewood and water, the march of the army should be regulated according to a schedule of short and long halts. Forage and provisions should be carried in double the quantity that may be required in any emergency. In the absence of separate means to carry rations, the army itself should be entrusted with the business of carrying them; or they may be stored in a central place.

The order of march should be: in front the leader (*náyaka*); in the centre the harem and the master (the king); on the sides horses and bodyguards (*báhútsára*); at the extremity of the (marching) circular-array, elephants and the surplus army; on all sides the army; and other troops following the camp.

The commissariat, the army of an ally, and his followers should select their own road: for armies who have secured suitable positions will prove superior in fight to those who are in bad positions.

The army of the lowest quality can march a *yojana* (8 kilometres a day); that of the middle quality a *yojana* and a half and the best army two *yojanas*. Hence, it is easy to ascertain the rate of march. The commander should march behind and put up his camp in the front.

In case of any obstruction, the army should march in crocodile array in the front, in cart-like array behind, and on the sides in diamond-like array (i.e., in four or five rows, each having its front, rear and sides) and in a compact array on all sides. When the army is marching on a path passable by a single man, it should march in pin-like array. When peace is made with one and war is to be waged with another, steps should be taken to protect the allies who are bringing help against enemies, such as an enemy in the rear, his ally, a *madhyama* king, or a neutral king. Roads with obstructions should be examined and cleared. Finance, the army, the strength of the armies of allies, enemies, and wild tribes, the prospect of rains, and the seasons should be thoroughly examined.

When the protective power of fortifications and stores (of the enemies) is on its decay, when it is thought that distress of the hired army or of an ally's army (of the enemy) is impending; when intriguers are not for a quick march; or when the enemy is likely to come to terms (with the invader), slow march should be made; otherwise quick march should be made. Waters may be crossed by means of elephants, planks spread over pillars erected, bridges, boats, timber and mass of bamboos, as well as by means of dry sour gourds, big baskets covered with skins, and rafts.

When the crossing of a river is obstructed by the enemy, the invader may cross it elsewhere together with his elephants and horses, and entangle the enemy in an ambush (*sattra*). He should protect his army when it has to pass a long desert without water; when it is without grass, firewood and water; when it has to traverse a difficult road; when it is harassed by an enemy's attacks; when it is suffering from hunger and thirst after a journey; when it is ascending or descending a mountainous country full of mire, water-pools, rivers and cataracts; when it finds itself crowded in a narrow and difficult path; when it is halting, starting or eating; when it is tired from a long march; when it is sleepy; when it is suffering from a disease, pestilence or famine; when a great portion of its infantry, cavalry and elephants is diseased; when it is not sufficiently strong; or when it is under troubles. He should destroy the enemy's army under such circumstances.

When the enemy's army is marching through a path traversable by a single man, the commander (of the invader's army) should ascertain its strength by estimating the quantity of food-stuffs, grass, bedding, and other requisites, fire pots (*agninidhána*), flags and weapons. He should also conceal those of his own army.

Forms of Treacherous Fights
Encouragement to One's Own Army
Fighting Between Armies

He who is possessed of a strong army, who has succeeded in his intrigues, and who has applied remedies against dangers may undertake an open fight, if he has secured a position favourable to himself; otherwise he should engage in a treacherous fight.

He should strike the enemy when the latter's army is under troubles or is furiously attacked. He who has secured a favourable position may strike the enemy entangled in an unfavourable position. He who possesses control over the elements of his own state may, through the aid of the enemy's traitors, enemies and inimical wild tribes, make a false impression of his own defeat on the mind of the enemy who is entrenched in a favourable position, and having thus dragged the enemy into an unfavourable position, he may strike the latter.

When the enemy's army is in a compact body, he should break it by means of his elephants. When the enemy has come down from its favourable position, following the false impression of the invader's defeat, the invader may turn back and strike the enemy's army, broken or unbroken. Having struck the front of the enemy's army, he may strike it again by means of his elephants and horses when it has shown its back and is running away. When frontal attack is unfavourable, he should strike it from behind. When an attack on the rear is unfavourable, he should strike it in front. When an attack on one side is unfavourable, he should strike it on the other.

Having caused the enemy to fight against his own army of traitors, enemies and wild tribes, the invader should, with his fresh army, strike the enemy when tired. Or having through the aid of the army of traitors given the enemy the impression of defeat, the invader with full confidence in his own strength may lure and strike the overconfident enemy. Or the invader, if he is vigilant, may strike the careless enemy when the latter is deluded with the thought that the invader's merchants, camp and carriers have been destroyed. Or having made his strong force look like a weak force, he may strike the enemy's brave men when falling against him. Or having captured the enemy's cattle or having destroyed the enemy's dogs (*svapadavadha*), he may induce the enemy's brave men to come out and may slay them. Or having made the enemy's men sleepless by harassing them at night, he may strike them during the day, when they are weary from want of sleep and are parched by heat, himself being under the shade. Or with his army of elephants enshrouded with cotton and leather dress, he may offer a night-battle to his enemy. Or he may strike the enemy's men during the afternoon when they are tired by making preparations during the forenoon; or he may strike the whole of the enemy's army when it is facing the sun.

A desert, marshes, mountains, valleys, uneven boats, cows, cart-like array of the army, mist, and night are *sattras* to lure the enemy.

The beginning of an attack is the time for treacherous fights. As to an open or fair fight, a virtuous king should call his army together, and, specifying the place and time of battle, address them. His minister and priest should encourage the army. Astrologers and other followers of the king should infuse spirit into the army by pointing out the impregnable nature of the array of the army, the king's power to associate with gods, and his omniscience; and they should at the same time frighten the enemy.

The day before the battle, the king should fast and lie down on his chariot with weapons. He should also make oblations into the fire pronouncing the *mantras* of the *Atharvaveda,* and cause prayers to be offered for the good of the victors as well as of those who attain to heaven by dying in battle. He should submit his person to Bráhmans; and have the central portion of his army consist of men noted for their bravery, skill, high birth, and loyalty and those who are not displeased with the rewards and honours bestowed on them. The place that is to be occupied by the king is that portion of the army which has his relatives and other men, skilled in using weapons, and having no flags and head-dress. He should mount an elephant or a chariot, if the army consists mostly of horses; or he may mount that kind of animal, of which the army is mostly composed or which is the most skilfully trained. One who is disguised like the king should attend to the work of arraying the army.

Soothsayers and court bards should describe heaven as the goal for the brave and hell for the timid; and also extol the caste, family, deeds, and character of his men. The followers of the priest should proclaim the auspicious aspects of the witchcraft performed. Spies, carpenters and astrologers should also declare the success of their own operations and the failure of those of the enemy.

After having pleased the army with rewards and honours, the commander-in-chief should address it and say: "A hundred thousand (*panas*) for slaying the king (the enemy); fifty thousand for slaying the commander-in-chief, and the heir-apparent; ten thousand for slaying the chief of the brave; five thousand for destroying an elephant, or a chariot; a thousand for killing a horse, a hundred (*panas*) for slaying the chief of the infantry; twenty for bringing a head; and twice the pay in addition to whatever is seized. This information should be made known to the leaders of every group of ten men. (*An annual salary of 60 panas could purchase grain, sufficient for four meals daily for one Arya male*).

Physicians with surgical instruments (*sastra*), machines, remedial oils, and cloth in their hands; and women with prepared food and beverage should stand behind, uttering encouraging words to the fighting men.

The army should be arrayed on a favourable position, facing other than the south, with its back turned to the sun, and capable to rush as it stands. If the array is made on an unfavourable spot, horses should charge. If the army arrayed on an unfavourable position is confined or is made to withdraw (by the enemy), it will be subjugated. The nature of the ground in the front, sides and the rear should be examined. On an even site, staff-like or circular array should be made; and on an uneven ground, arrays of compact movement or of detached bodies should be made.

Having broken the whole army (of the enemy), (the invader) should seek for peace. If the armies are of equal strength, he should make peace when requested for it. If the enemy's army is inferior, he should attempt to destroy it, but not that which has secured a favourable position and is reckless of life.

Battlefields

The Work of Infantry, Cavalry, Chariots, and Elephants

Favourable positions for infantry, cavalry, chariots, and elephants are desirable both for war and camp. For men who are trained to fight in desert tracts, forests, valleys, or plains, and for those who are trained to fight from ditches or heights, during the day or night, and for elephants which are bred in countries with rivers, mountains, marshy lands, or lakes, as well as for horses, such battlefields as they would find suitable, are to be secured. For elephants, horses and men, even or uneven ground is good, either for war or for camp.

That ground which is even, firm, free from mounds and pits made by wheels and foot-prints of beasts, not offering obstructions to the axle, free from trees, plants, creepers and trunks of trees, not wet, and free from pits, ant-hills, sand, and thorns is the ground for chariots. Also, ground which is free from mounds and wet lands, and which affords space for turning is an excellent ground for chariots.

That which contains small stones, trees and pits that can be jumped over and which is almost free from thorns, is expansive, free from mud, water and roots of trees, and which is devoid of piercing gravel is suitable ground for horses.

Ground, which is free from thorns, is not very uneven, but very expansive with big stones, with dry or green trees and ant-hills is suitable ground for the infantry.

Ground which is uneven with assailable hills and valleys, which has trees that can be pulled down and plants that can be torn, and which is full of muddy soil free from thorns is suitable ground for elephants. Also ground which has dust, muddy soil, water, grass and weeds, and which is free from thorns (known as dog's teeth) and obstructions from the branches of big trees is an excellent ground for elephants.

Tasks of the cavalry include destruction or protection of the commissariat and of troops arriving afresh; supervision of the discipline of the army; protecting the flanks of the army; first attack; dispersion of the enemy's army; carrying the treasury and the princes; falling against the rear of the enemy; chasing the timid; pursuit; and concentration.

The tasks of the elephants include marching in the vanguard; preparing the roads, camping grounds and paths; protecting flanks; forced entrance into impregnable places; the subjugation of one of the four constituents of the army; breaking a compact army; protection against dangers; trampling down the enemy's army; destruction of walls, gates and towers; and carrying the treasury.

The tasks of chariots include protection of the army; repelling attacks; seizing and abandoning positions during battle; gathering a dispersed army; breaking the compact array of the enemy's army; frightening it; magnificence; and fearful noise.

The tasks of infantry are the carrying of weapons, and fighting.

The Distinctive Array of Troops in Respect of Wings, Flanks, and Front

Distinction between Strong and Weak Troops

Battle with Infantry, Cavalry, Chariots and Elephants

Having fortified a camp at the distance of five hundred bows the commander-in-chief (*senapati)* should begin to fight. Having detached a strong reserve and kept it on a favourable position, not visible to the enemy, the commander-in-chief should array the rest of the army. The infantry should be arrayed such that the space between any two men is a *sama* (14 *angulas* or one foot); cavalry with three *samas*; chariots with four *samas;* and elephants with twice or thrice as much space as between any two chariots. With such an array free to move and having no confusion, one should fight.

A bow means five *aratnis* (5 × 24 = 120 *angulas*). Archers should be stationed at the distance of five bows from one line to another; the cavalry at the distance of three bows; and chariots or elephants at the distance of five bows.

The intervening space (*aníkasandhi*) between wings, flanks and front of the army should be five bows. There must be three men to oppose a horse (*pratiyoddha*); fifteen men or five horses to oppose a chariot or an elephant; and as many as fifteen servants (*pádagopa)* for a horse, a chariot and an elephant should be maintained.

Three groups (*aníka*) of three chariots each should be stationed in front; the same number on the two flanks and the two wings. Thus, in an array of chariots, the number of chariots amounts to forty-five, two hundred and twenty-five horses, six hundred and seventy-five men, and as many servants to attend upon the horses, chariots and elephants—this is called an even array of troops. The number of chariots in this array (of three groups of three chariots each) may be increased by two and two till the increased number amounts to twenty-one. Thus, this array of odd numbers of chariots gives rise to ten odd varieties. Thus the surplus of the army may therefore be distributed in the above manner. Two-thirds of the (surplus) chariots may be added to the flanks and the wings, the rest being put in front. Thus the added surplus of chariots should be one-third less than the number added to the flanks and wings. As many horses, chariots, and elephants may be added without having occasion to cause confusion in fighting.

An array of elephants, chariots, and horses mixed together may also be made: at the extremities of the circle (array). The array in which the front is occupied by elephants, the flanks by chariots, and the wings by horses is an array which can break the centre of the enemy's army; the reverse of this can harass the extremities of the enemy's army. An array of elephants may also be made: the front by such elephants as are trained for war; the flanks by such as are trained for riding; and the wings by rogue elephants.

In an array of horses, the front horses must have mail armour; and the flanks and wings have horses without armour. In an array of infantry, men dressed in mail armour must be in front, archers in the rear, and men without armour on the wings; or horses on the wings, elephants on the flanks, and chariots in front; other changes may also be made so as to oppose the enemy's army successfully.

The best army is that which consists of strong infantry and of such elephants and horses as are noted for their breed, birth, strength, youth, vitality, capacity to run even in old age, fury, skill, firmness, magnanimity, obedience, and good habits.

One-third of the best of infantry, cavalry and elephants should be kept in front; two-thirds on both the flanks and wings; the array of the army according to the strength of its constituents is in the direct order; that which is arrayed mixing one-third of strong and weak troops is in the reverse order. Thus, one should know all the varieties of arraying the array.

Having stationed the weak troops at the extremities, they could be pliable to the force of the enemy's onslaught. Having stationed the strength of the army in front, one should make the wings equally strong. One-third of the best should be kept in the rear, and weak troops in the centre—this array is able to resist the enemy. Having made an array, he should strike the enemy with one or two of the divisions on the wings, flanks, and front, and capture the enemy by means of the rest of the troops.

When the enemy's force is weak, with few horses and elephants, and is contaminated with the intrigue of treacherous ministers, the conqueror should strike it with his best troops. He should increase the numerical strength of that constituent of the army which is physically weak. He should array his troops on that side on which the enemy is weak or from which danger is apprehended.

Running against; running round; running beyond; running back; disturbing the enemy's halt; gathering the troops; curving, circling, miscellaneous operations; removal of the rear; pursuit of the line from the front, flanks and rear; protection of the broken army; and falling upon the broken army—these are the forms of waging war with horses.

The destruction of the four constituents of the army, either single or combined; the dispersion of the flanks, wings and front trampling down; and attacking the army when it is asleep—these are the varieties of waging war with elephants.

The same varieties with the exception of disturbing the enemy's halt; running against; running back; and fighting from where it stands on its own ground are the varieties of waging war with chariots.

Striking in all places and at all times and striking by surprise is the manner of waging war with infantry.

In this way, the commander-in-chief should make odd or even arrays, keeping the strength of the four constituents of the army equal. Having gone to a distance of 200 bows, the king should take his position together with the reserve of his army. He should never attempt to fight without a reserve force, for it is by the reserve force that dispersed troops are collected together.

The Arrays of the Army against an Enemy

The principal formations (arrays) of the army are:

- Stationing the army so as to stand abreast, is a staff-like array (*danda*). It has equal strength on its wings, flanks and front. The same array is called *pradara* (breaking the enemy's array) when its flanks are made to project in front. It is called *dridhaka* (firm) when its wings and flanks are stretched back and *asahya* (irresistible) when its wings are lengthened. When, having formed the wings, the front is made to bulge out, it is called an eagle-like array. The same four varieties are called "a bow," "the centre of a bow," "a hold," and "a stronghold," when they are arranged in a reverse form. That, of which the wings are arrayed like a bow, is called *sanjaya* (victory). The same with projected front is called *vijaya* (conqueror); that which has its flanks and wings formed like a staff is called *sthúlakarna* (big ear); the same with its front made twice as strong as the conqueror, is called *visálavijaya* (vast victory); that which has its wings stretched forward is called *chamúmukha* (face of the army); and the same is called *ghashásya* (face of the fish) when it is arrayed in the reverse form.

- Stationing the army in a line so that one may follow the other, is a snake-like array (*bhoga*). The snake-like array in which the wings, flanks and front are of unequal depth is called *sarpasári* (serpentine movement), or *gomútrika* (the course of a cow's urine). When it consists of two lines in front and has its wings arranged as in the staff-like array, it is called a cart-like array; the reverse of this is called a crocodile-like array; the cart-like array which consists of elephants, horses and chariots is called *váripatantaka*
- Stationing the army so as to face all the directions is a circle array (*mandala*). The circle-like array in which the distinction of wings, flanks and front is lost is called *sarvatomukha* (facing all directions), or *sarvatobhadra* (all auspicious), *ashtáníka* (one of eight divisions), or *vijaya* (victory).
- A detached arrangement of the army into small bodies so as to enable each to act for itself, is termed an array in detached order (*asamhata*). When five divisions of the army are arranged in detached order, it is called *vajra* (diamond), or *godha* (alligator); when four divisions, it is called *udyánaka* (park), or *kákapadi* (crow's foot); when three divisions, it is called a*rdhachandrika* (half-moon).

The sequence of an attack should be with infantry, cavalry, chariots and then elephants.

For every ten members of each of the constituents of the army, there must be one commander, called *padika*; ten *padikas* under a *senápati*; ten *senápatis* under a náyaka, (leader).

The constituents of the array of the army should be called after the names of trumpet sounds, flags and ensigns. Achievement of success in arranging the constituents of the army, in gathering the forces, in camping, in marching, in turning back, in making onslaughts, and in the array of equal strength depends upon the place and time of action.

CONDUCT OF WAR

The Knowledge of Power, Place, Time, Strength, and Weakness

The conqueror should know the comparative strength and weakness of himself and of his enemy; and having ascertained the power, place, time, the time of marching and of recruiting the army, the consequences, the loss of men and money, and profits and danger, he should march with his full force; otherwise, he should keep quiet.

A ruler who is possessed of power overreaches, by the sheer force of his power, another who is merely enthusiastic. Having acquired, captured, or bought another enthusiastic ruler as well as brave soldiers, he can have an army of horses, elephants, chariots, and others to move anywhere without impediment. Powerful rulers have conquered the earth by winning over or purchasing the aid of spirited and motivated persons.

A ruler, possessed of skill for intrigue (*mantrasakti*) and with an eye for knowledge who is acquainted with the science of polity can with little effort make use of his skill and succeed by means of conciliation and other strategic means and by spies and chemical appliances in over-reaching even those rulers who are possessed of enthusiasm and power. Thus of the three acquirements, viz., enthusiasm, power and skill for intrigue, he who possesses more of the latter quality will be successful in over-reaching others.

The thousand *yojanas* of the northern portion of the country that stretches between the Himalayas and the ocean form the dominion of no insignificant emperor. In it there are such varieties of land, as forests, villages, level plains, and uneven grounds. In such lands, the conqueror should undertake such works as he considers conducive to his power and prosperity. That part of the country, in which his army finds a convenient place for its manoeuvres and which is unfavourable to his enemy, is the best to wage war.

The Time of Invasion

Time consists of cold, hot, and rainy periods. The divisions of time are: the night, the day, the fortnight, the month, the season, solstices, the year, and the *yuga* (cycle of five years). In these divisions of time he should undertake such works as are conducive to the growth of his power and prosperity. That time which is congenial for the manoeuvre of his army, but which is of the reverse nature for his enemy is the best.

Strength, place, and time, are complementary to each other. Whoever is possessed of these three should, after having placed one-third or one fourth of his army to protect his base of operations against his rear-enemy and wild tribes in his vicinity and after having taken with him as much army and treasure as is sufficient to accomplish his work, march during the month of *Márgásírsha* (December) against his enemy whose collection of grain is old and insipid and who has also not repaired his fortifications, in order to destroy the enemy's rainy season and autumnal crops (*mushti*). He should march during the month of *Chaitra* (March), if he means to destroy the enemy's autumnal and spring crops. He should march during the month of *Jyestha* (May-June) against one whose storage of fodder, firewood and water has diminished and who has not repaired his fortifications. He may march during the dewy season against a country which is of hot climate and in which fodder and water are obtained in little quantities. He may march during the summer against a country in which the sun is enshrouded by mist and which is full of deep valleys and thickets of trees and grass. He may march during the rains against a country which is suitable for the manoeuvre of his own army and which is of the reverse nature for his enemy's army. He should consider undertaking long marches in the months of December and January, a march of average length between March and April, and short marches between May and June.

When a ruler's resources are sufficient he should campaign, even if the troubles of an enemy cannot be properly assessed. When the weather is free from heat, in a country containing plenty of water and during the rainy season, one should march with an army mostly composed of elephants. Against a country of the reverse description, i.e., which as little rain and muddy water, one should march with an army mostly composed of asses, camels, and horses.

In a desert, one should march during the rainy season with all the four constituents of the army (elephants, horses, chariots, and men). One should prepare a schedule of short and long distances to be marched in accordance with the nature of the ground to be traversed. When the task to be accomplished is small, marches against all kinds of enemies should be of short duration; and when it is great, it should also be of long duration.

The Time of Recruiting the Army

When a ruler thinks that his army is more than he requires for the defence of his own possessions or when he thinks that some of them may be disaffected; or when he thinks that his enemy has a strong army and is, therefore, to be fought with much skill; or when he thinks that though the roads are good and the weather favourable, it is his army that can endure wear and tear; or when he thinks that hired soldiers and other kinds of troops cannot be relied upon lest they might lend their ears to the intrigues of the enemy to be invaded; or when he thinks that other kinds of force are wanting in strength, then is the time for taking the army on a campaign.

When a ruler thinks that the army he has hired is greater than his intrinsic army; that his enemy's army is small and disaffected, insignificant and weak; that actual fighting would be less than a treacherous fight; that the area to be traversed and the time required do not entail much loss; and that his own army is well-trained, beyond the fear of intrigue and is reliable; then is the time for leading the hired army.

When a ruler thinks that his corps of soldiers can be trusted both to defend his country and to march against his enemy; that he has to be absent only for a short time; or that his enemy's army consists mostly of soldiers affected by mortmain, and that the enemy is desirous of a treacherous fight rather than an actual war, then is the time for the enlistment of soldiers (*srení*).

When a ruler thinks that the strong help he has in his ally can be made use of both in his own country and in his marches; that he has to be absent only for a short time, and actual fight is more than treacherous fight; that having made his ally's army to occupy wild tracts, cities, or plains and to fight with the enemy's ally, he, himself, should lead his own army to fight with the enemy's army; that his work can be accomplished by his ally as well; that his success depends on his ally; that he has a ally near and deserving of obligation; or that he has to utilize the excessive force of his ally, then is the time for the enlistment of a ally's army.

When a ruler thinks that he will have to make his strong enemy to fight against another enemy on account of a city, a plain, or a wild tract of land, and that in that fight he will achieve one or the other of his objects, just like an outcast person in the fight between a dog and a pig; that through the battle, he will have the mischievous power of his enemy's allies destroyed; that he will have to make his immediate and powerful enemy march elsewhere and thus get rid of internal rebellion which his enemy might have occasioned; and that the time of battle between enemies or between inferior rulers has arrived, then is the time for the exercise of an enemy's forces.

When a ruler thinks that an army of wild tribes is on the same route that his enemy has to traverse; that the route is unfavourable for the march of his enemy's army; that his enemy's army consists mostly of wild tribes; that just as a wood-apple (*bilva*) is broken by means of another wood-apple, and the small army of his enemy is to be destroyed, then is the time for engaging the army of wild tribes. One has to pay the army of wild tribes either with raw produce or with allowance for plunder.

That army which is vast and composed of various kinds of enthusiastic soldiers who rise even without provision and wages for plunder when told or untold; that which is capable of applying its own remedies against unfavourable rains; that which can be disbanded and which is invincible for enemies; and that, of which all the men are of the same country, same caste, and same training, is a compact body of vast power.

When the time for the march of the enemy's army has approached, one has to obstruct the enemy or make his movements fruitless, or, by false promise, cause him to delay the march, and then deceive him after the time for his march has passed. One should ever be vigilant to increase one's own resources and frustrate the attempts of the enemy to gain in strength.

The Form of Equipment

A structured army is better than a hired army inasmuch as the existence of the former is dependent on that of its master, and is constantly drilled. A corps of soldiers which is native, which has the same end in view as the ruler, and which is actuated with similar feelings of rivalry, anger, and expectation of success and gain, is better than the army of a ally. Even that corps of soldiers which is further removed in place and time is better than the army of a ally.

The army of an enemy under the leadership of an *Arya* is better than an army of wild tribes. Both of them (the army of an enemy and of wild tribes) are anxious for plunder. In the absence of plunder and under troubles, they prove as dangerous as a lurking snake.

An army may be composed of *Bráhmans, Kshatriyas, Vaisyas*, or *Súdras*, but the enemy may win over to himself an army of *Bráhmans* by means of prostration. Hence, an army of *Kshatriyas* trained in the art of wielding weapons is better; or the army of *Vaisyas* or *Súdras* having great numerical strength is better. Hence one should recruit an army considering the nature and organisation of the army of the enemy.

The army which possesses elephants, machines, *sakatagarbha* (?), *kunta* (a wooden rod), *prása* (a twin-handled short sword), *kharvataka* (?), bamboo sticks and iron rods can oppose an army of elephants. The same possessed of stones, clubs, armour, hooks, and spears in plenty can oppose an army of chariots or cavalry.

The Work of Arraying a Rival Force

Soldiers, clad in armour, can oppose elephants but they can be opposed men by cavalry. Soldiers, clad in armour, with chariots, possessing defensive weapons, and infantry can oppose an army consisting of all the four constituents (elephants, chariots, cavalry and infantry). Thus considering the strength of the constituents of one's own quadripartite army, one should recruit men to it so as to oppose an enemy's army successfully.

Consideration of Annoyance in the Rear

Of the two, slight annoyance in the rear, and considerable profit in the front, slight annoyance in the rear is more serious. Traitors, enemies, and wild tribes augment the slight annoyance which one may have in the rear. The members of one's own state may be provoked about the acquisition of considerable profit in the front.

When one under the protection of another has come to such a condition (i.e., slight annoyance in the rear and considerable profit in the front), then one should endeavour to cause to the rear enemy the loss and impoverishment of his servants and allies; and in order to fetch the profit in the front, one should employ the commander of the army or the heir-apparent to lead the army.

The ruler himself may go in person to receive the profit in the front, if he is able to ward off the annoyance in the rear. If he is apprehensive of internal troubles, he may take with him the suspected leaders. If he is apprehensive of external troubles, he should march after keeping in his capital (as hostages) the sons and wives of suspected enemies; and after having split into a number of divisions the troops of the officer in charge of waste lands (*súnyapála*) and having placed those divisions under the command of several chiefs. Else, he may abandon his march, for it has been already stated that internal troubles are more serious than external troubles.

Remedies against Internal and External Troubles

Provocation of any minister, the priest, the commander-in-chief, and the heir-apparent is what is termed internal trouble. The ruler should get rid of such an internal enemy either by owning up his own fault or by pointing out the danger arising from an external enemy. When the priest is guilty of the gravest treason, relief should be found either by confining him or by banishing him. When the heir-apparent is guilty, confinement or death (*nigraha*) can be sentenced, provided that there is another son of good character. From these, the case of the minister and the commander-in-chief is explained.

When a son, or a brother, or any other person of the royal family attempts to seize the kingdom, he should be won over by holding out promises. When this is not possible, he should be conciliated by allowing him to enjoy what he has already seized, or by making an agreement with him, or by means of intrigue through an enemy, or by securing to him land from an enemy. Or he may be sent out on a mission with an inimical force to receive the only punishment he deserves; or a conspiracy may be made with a frontier ruler or wild tribes whose displeasure he has incurred; or the same policy that is employed in securing an imprisoned prince or in seizing an enemy's villages may be resorted to.

The provocation of the chief of a district (*ráshtramukhya*), the officer in charge of the boundary, the chief of wild tribes, and a conquered ruler is what is termed external trouble. This should be overcome by setting one against the other. Whoever among these has strongly fortified himself should be caught hold of through the agency of a frontier ruler, or the chief of wild tribes, or a scion of his family, or an imprisoned prince; or he may be captured through an ally, so that he may not combine with an enemy; or a spy may prevent him from combining with an enemy by warning him of the dangers of being double-crossed. The spy should however appoint some persons to murder him.

In the case of a person who is capable of causing or alleviating troubles, intrigue should be made use of; and in the case of a person who is of reliable character, able to undertake tasks, and to favour his ally in his success, and to afford protection against calamities, counter-intrigue (*pratijápa*) should be made use of. It should also be considered whether the person is of good disposition or of obstinate temper (*satha*).

When a person of good disposition makes a conspiracy for the purpose of acquiring what is to be enjoyed by both then an agreement should be made with him. But when a person of obstinate temper so conspires, he should be allowed to have his own way and then deceived. Thus the form of policy to be adopted should be considered.

Consideration about Loss of Men, Wealth and Profit

Loss of trained men is what is called *kshaya*. Diminution of gold and grains is loss of wealth. When the expected profit overweighs both these; then one should march against an enemy.

The characteristics of an expected profit are: that which is receivable, that which is to be returned, that which pleases all, that which incites hatred, that which is realised in a short time, that which entails little loss of men to earn, that which entails little loss of wealth to earn, that which is vast, that which is productive, that which is harmless, that which is just, and that which comes first.

When a profit is easily acquired and secured without the necessity of returning it, it is termed 'receivable'; that which is of the reverse nature is 'repayable.' Whoever receives a repayable profit or enjoys it invites destruction. A repayable profit is only taken when he thinks that by taking it I shall cause my enemy's treasury, army, and other defensive resources to dwindle; or I shall set my enemy against another enemy; or that a person will be a lasting ally of mine.

The profit which a virtuous ruler receives from a wicked ruler pleases both his own and other people; that which is of the reverse nature excites hatred. Profit which is received at the advice of ministers incites hatred.

Profit acquired by mere marching is what is acquired soon. That which is realised by negotiation (*mantrasáddhya*) entails little loss of men. That which requires merely the expenditure of provisions entails little loss of wealth. That which is immediately of considerable value is vast. That which is the source of wealth is productive. That which is attained with no troubles is harmless. That which is acquired justly without any hindrance from allies is best.

When profits (from two sources) are equal, he should consider the place and time, the strength and means (required to acquire it), affection and disaffection (caused by it), intrigue and absence of intrigue (involving it), its proximity and distance, its present and future effects, it's worth, quantity and usefulness. A ruler should accept only that profit which is possessed of most of the aforesaid good characteristics.

Obstructions to profit are: passion, anger, timidity, mercy, bashfulness, living like one who is not an *Arya*, haughtiness, pity, desire for the other world, strict adherence to a virtuous life, deception, neediness, envy, negligence of what is at hand, generosity, want of faith, fear, and faith in the auspiciousness of lunar days and stars. Wealth will pass away from that childish man who inquires most after the stars; for, if wealth is the star for wealth; what will the stars do?

External and Internal Dangers

The formation of a treaty and other settlements other than they ought to be made is bad policy. From it arise dangers.

Where foreigners carry on an intrigue with local men or local men with foreigners, the consequence of the intrigue will be very serious. Abettors of an intrigue have a better chance of success than its originators. When the originators of an intrigue are put down, others will hardly succeed. When local persons are abetting (with foreigners), the means to be employed to suppress them are conciliation (*sáma*) and gifts (*dána*).

The act of pleasing a man with a high rank and honour is conciliation; favour and remission of taxes or employment to conduct state-works is what is termed gifts. When foreigners are abetting, the ruler should employ the policy of dissension and coercion. Spies under the guise of friends may inform on foreigners. Spies under the garb of traitors may mix with traitors and separate them from foreigners, or foreigners from local traitors. Spies may make friendship with traitors and kill them with weapons or poison; or having invited plotting foreigners, they may murder them.

Where foreigners carry on an intrigue with foreigners, or local men with local men, the consequences of the intrigue, unanimously carried on with a set purpose, will be very serious. When guilt is got rid of, there will be no guilty persons; but when a guilty person is got rid of, the guilt will contaminate others. Hence, when foreigners carry on an intrigue, the ruler should employ the policy of dissension and coercion. Spies may mix with the servants and soldiers of the abettor (of foreign conspirators) and kill them with weapons, poison, and other means. Other spies may then expose or betray the abettor.

When local men carry on an intrigue with local men, the ruler should employ necessary strategic means to put it down. He may employ the policy of conciliation with regard to those who keep the appearance of contentment, or who are naturally discontented or otherwise. Gifts may be given under the pretext of having been satisfied with a favoured man's steadfastness in maintaining the purity of his character, or under the plea of anxious care about his woe.

Persons Associated With Traitors and Enemies

There are two kinds of innocent persons, those who have disassociated themselves from traitors and those who have kept themselves away from enemies. In order to separate citizens and country-people from traitors, the ruler should employ all strategic means, except coercion. It is very difficult to inflict punishment on an assembly of influential men; and if inflicted at all, it may not produce the desired effect, but may give rise to undesirable consequences. He may, however, take steps against the leaders of the seditious.

In order to separate his people from an enemy, he should employ conciliation and other strategic means to frustrate the attempt of those who are the enemy's principal agents or by who the enemy's work is to be carried out. Success in securing the services of capable agents depends upon the ruler; success of efforts depends upon ministers; and success to be achieved through capable agents is, therefore, dependent both upon the ruler and his ministers.

When an ally does not come to terms, intrigue should be resorted to. Through spies, the ally should be won over after separating him from the enemy. Or attempts may be made to win him over who is the last among combined allies; for when he who is the last among combined allies is secured, those who occupy the middle rank will be separated from each other; or attempts may be made to win over an ally who occupies middle rank; for when an ally occupying middle rank among combined rulers is secured, allies occupying the extreme ranks cannot keep the union.

When any two rulers are apprehensive of enmity and seizure of land from each other, seeds of dissension may be sown between them. The timid of the two may be threatened with destruction.

When from one's own country or from another's country merchandise or commodities for manufacture are going to an enemy's country, spies may spread the information that those commodities are obtained from one whom the enemy wanted to march against. The conqueror may gather some merchandise peculiar to his enemy's country and unknown elsewhere. Spies, under the garb of merchants, may sell that merchandise to other important enemies and tell them that that merchandise was given (to the conqueror) by the enemy (whose country's product it is).

Or having pleased with wealth and honour those who are highly treacherous (among an enemy's people), the conqueror may cause them to live with the enemy, armed with weapons, poison and fire. One of the ministers of the enemy may be killed. His sons and wife may be induced to say that the minister was killed at night (by such and such a person). Then the enemy's minister may ask every one of the family of the murdered minister (as to the cause of the death). If they say in reply as they are told, they may be caused to be set free; if they do not do so, they may be caused to be caught hold of. Whoever has gained the confidence of the ruler may tell the ruler (the enemy) that he (the enemy) has to guard his own person from such and such a minister. Then the recipient of salaries from the two states (the conqueror's and the enemy's state) may inform the suspected minister to destroy (the ruler). Likewise seeds of dissension may be sown among combined states.

Spies under concealment may, without help murder by means of weapons, poison or other things a fortified enemy who is of mean character or who is under troubles; any one of hidden spies may do the work when it is found easy; or an ardent spy alone may do the work by means of weapons, poison or fire; for an ardent spy can do what others require aids to do.

There are four forms of strategic means against enemies, in order of usage:

- Conciliation (*sama*)
- Gifts (*dana*)
- Dissension (*bhed*)
- Coercion (*danda*)

The same means are employed in the case of local enemies too. When the country is full of local enemies, they may be got rid of by making them drink poisonous liquids). An obstinate or clever enemy may be destroyed by spies or by means of poison given to him in good faith.

Doubts about Wealth and Harm

Intensity of desire and other passions provoke one's own people; bad policies provoke external enemies. Both these are the characteristics of a devilish life. Anger disturbs the feelings of one's own men. Wealth is conducive to the prosperity of one's enemy and can be dangerous and provocative wealth.

Wealth which, when obtained, increases the enemy's prosperity, or which, though obtained, is repayable to the enemy, or which causes loss of men and money, is dangerous wealth. Wealth which is enjoyed in common by neighbouring rulers and which is acquired at their expense; or wealth which is asked for by an enemy; or wealth which is seized like one's own property; or wealth which is acquired in the front and which causes future troubles or provokes an enemy in the rear; or wealth which is obtained by destroying an ally or by breaking a treaty and which is therefore detested by the Circle of States are examples of dangerous wealth.

Wealth which causes fear from one's own people or from an enemy is provocative wealth. There are the six varieties of harmful wealth, in order of preference:

- Wealth productive of wealth; i.e. destruction of an enemy in the front resulting in the destruction of an enemy in the rear.
- Wealth productive of nothing; i.e. that acquired by helping a neutral ruler with the army.
- Wealth productive of harm; i.e. reduction of the internal strength of an enemy
- Loss or harm productive of wealth; i.e. helping the neighbouring ruler of an enemy with men and money
- Sustenance of harm for no profit; i.e. withdrawal after encouraging or setting a ruler of poor resources (against another)
- Harm productive of harm; i.e. inactivity after inciting a superior ruler

When there is reason to apprehend fear from enemies on all sides, it is a dangerous trouble. When an ally comes forward to avert this fear, that trouble becomes involved in doubt. In these two cases, success can be achieved by securing the support of a nomadic enemy and the enemy of the rear-enemy.

When the prospect of acquiring profit from one or the other side is irremediably obstructed by enemies, it is called "dangerous wealth." In this case as well as in the case of profit from all sides, one should undertake to march for acquiring profitable wealth. When the prospects of getting wealth (from two sides) are equal, one should march to secure that which is important, near, unfailing, and obtainable by easy means.

When there is the apprehension of harm from one quarter as well as from another, it is wealth beset with danger from two sides. In this case as well as in the case of wealth involved in danger from all sides, success is to be desired with the help of allies. In the absence of allies, the ruler should attempt to ward off harm from one side with the help of an ally who can be easily won over; he should ward off harm from two sides with help of an ally of superior power; and he should ward off harm from all sides with all the resources he can command. When it is impossible to do this, he should run away, leaving all that belongs to him; for if he lives, his return to power is certain.

When there is the prospect of wealth from one side and the apprehension of an attack from another, it is termed a situation beset with wealth and harm. In this case, the ruler should march to acquire that wealth which will enable him to ward off the attack; otherwise he should attempt to avert the attack.

When there is the apprehension of harm from one side and when the prospect of acquiring wealth from another side is involved in doubt, the ruler should ward off the harm first; when this is done, he should attempt to acquire the doubtful wealth.

When there is the prospect of wealth from one side and the apprehension of doubtful harm from another, it is a doubtful situation of harm and wealth from two sides. In this, he should attempt to ward off the doubts of harm against each of the elements of his sovereignty in order; for it is better to leave an ally under circumstances of doubtful harm, than the army. Also, the army may be left under circumstances of doubtful harm, but not the treasury. When all the elements of his sovereignty cannot be relieved from harm, he should attempt to relieve some of them at least. Among the elements, he should attempt to relieve first those animate elements which are most loyal, and free from greedy men. Of inanimate elements he should relieve that which is most precious and useful.

Since doubts of wealth and harm are constantly associated with all expeditions, it is better to secure wealth by which it is easy to destroy an enemy in the rear and his allies, to recoup the loss of men and money, to make provisions during the time of sojourning abroad, to make good what is repayable, and to defend the state. Also harm or doubtful prospects of wealth in one's own state are always intolerable.

At the close of an expedition, it is better to acquire wealth either by reducing or destroying a reducible or assailable enemy than to get into a situation of doubtful harm, lest enemies might cause troubles. But, for one who is not the leader of combination of states, it is better to risk the situation of doubtful wealth or harm in the middle or at the close of an expedition, since one is not obliged to continue the expedition.

Wealth, virtue, and enjoyment form the aggregate of the three kinds of wealth. Of these, it is better to secure wealth. Wealth or harm, virtue or sin, and enjoyment or grief, are the aggregate of the three kinds of doubts. Of these, it is better to try that which is mentioned first.

Success by the Employment of Alternative Strategic Means

In the case of troubles from sons, brothers or relatives, it is better to secure relief by means of conciliation and gifts. In the case of troubles from citizens or chiefs of the army, it is by means of gifts and sowing the seeds of dissension. In the case of troubles from a neighbouring ruler or wild tribes, it is by means of sowing the seeds of dissension and coercion.

Success against allies and enemies is always achieved by complicated means; for strategic means help each other. In the case of suspected ministers of an enemy, the employment of conciliation does not need the use of the other means; in the case of treacherous ministers it is by means of gifts; in the case of combination of states, it is by means of sowing the seeds of dissension; and in the case of the powerful, it is by means of coercion. When grave and light dangers are together apprehended, a particular means, or alternative means or all the means may be employed.

There are fifteen kinds of strategic means: When a ruler attains success by only one means among these various means, he is called one of single success; when by two, one of double success; when by three, one of treble success; and when by four, one of four-fold success.

As virtue is the basis of wealth and enjoyment is the end of wealth, success in achieving that kind of wealth which promotes virtue, wealth and enjoyment is termed success in all (*sarvárthasiddhi*).

SYNTHESIS

Introduction

The *Arthaśāstra* of Kautilya is generally construed to be a treatise on economics and particularly dealing with finances. From ancient times the population on the Indian sub-continent largely depended for their livelihood and sustenance on agriculture, cattle rearing and trade. In the Indian tradition, *Arth* been regarded as one of the three goals of human existence, the other two being, *Dharma* and *Kama*. In this connection, *Artha* is traditionally understood to stand for material well-being, as well as the means for securing wealth for a healthy social order. Like the other two goals, *Artha* has an all pervading concern with the life of an individual who has to pursue wealth as one of the goals of his life, and this cannot be achieved without security and livelihood.

Kautilya may have put together these precepts and the *Arthaśāstra* may be the culmination of a long period of analysis and not it's starting point. Kautilya's *Arthaśāstra* contains fifteen *adhikaranas* or books. Of these, the first five books deal with *tantra* or the internal administration of the state. The next eight books deal with *avapa* or its relation with the neighbouring states; and the last two are miscellaneous in character. In the sixth *adhikarna* the qualities which make each of the seven *prakritis* or constituents of the state are enumerated. The *Rajamandala* or the Circle of Kings as a preliminary to a discussion on the state's relations with its neighbours is also discussed.

The seventh *adhinkarna* describes the way in which each of the six *gunas* or measures of foreign policy may be used in various situations that are likely to arise. In the eighth *adhikarna* the calamities or weakness affecting the various constituents are described. The ninth and tenth *adhikarna*s deals with the army, mobilisation and conduct of expeditions, the eleventh *adikarna* describes how the would-be conqueror should subjugate independent oligarchic principalities. The twelfth *adhikarna* describes how a powerless king, when threatened by a stronger king, could frustrate the latter's design and ultimately overcome him. The thirteenth *adhikarna* concerns the conquest of the enemy's capital by subterfuge or fighting.

The well-being of the people, in general, was to be pursued and preserved. As an individual could not do it by himself without the assistance of the administration of the state, he delegated this vital task to the state, vis-a-vis its administration. In consequence, this aspect has become the most essential function of the state and statecraft. As contemplated by the tenets of *Arthaśāstra*, in addition to the protection of the earth and its inhabitants, the acquisition of territory and the concomitant protection of the population of the acquired territory became the ardent and sacred duty of the state. Thus, the composite science of *Arthaśāstra* encompasses all state functions cumulatively responsible for the well-being of the people, which was entirely the state responsibility. The welfare of the state also depends on an active foreign policy.

This implies that *Arthaśāstra* has a two-fold aim. First, it seeks to show that the ruler should protect his territory through proper administration of the state. Second, it denotes how territory should be conquered, and provided with a benevolent and wholesome administration for the general benefit of the inhabitants. Both these aims were altruistic as well as mandatory. These precepts were necessarily concerned with the internal as well as external policies of the state and, therefore, the *Arthaśāstra* extensively dealt with them. It is also concerned with politics, sociology, administration and the system of justice, both civil and criminal, and the attendant penalties/punishment to the aberrant citizen.

Abreast these concerns, there necessarily followed methods of defence, offence and warfare strategies, including espionage and counterespionage. However, conquest of territories outside the territorial and then-known geographical borders of India was deprecated. This sense of justice prevented any Indian king from attempting any conquest beyond the limits of India. It explains why Indian kings did not invade other countries as was done by the Muslims and Christians.

Arthaśāstra and Foreign Policy

The largest sections of *Arthaśāstra* cover diplomacy and warfare. Kautilya advocates prudence in pursuing the two basic foreign policy aims: securing the state's security against foreign aggression and expanding the state at the expense of other states. To these ends, diplomacy and intelligence or covert operations are preferable to waging war. Employing guile in statecraft is better than fixating on military force. The ruler and his advisers must carefully calculate the correlation of forces before launching war. Short-term gains through immediate action must be balanced against long-term gains by waiting for the right moment to act.

Kautilya speaks of seven constituent elements of the state. The *Swami* or the ruler, *Amatya*, the minister, *Janapada* the territory with people settled on it, *Durga*, the fortified capital, *Danda,* the army and *Mitra* the ally. The first six are the essential elements and the last in the list, viz. the ally is the ruler of a different similarly organised state and forms no part of the other state's internal organisation.

This mention is primarily in connection with that state's foreign policy. This doctrine of the *prakritis* makes no direct mention of the citizen of the state but the *janapada* refers to the territory of the state with people in it. The components are enumerated in the order of their relative importance.

Kautilya also lists out the *vyasanas* (calamities) that can befall the components of the state. The relative importance of the component of the state is based on the fact that if a *vyasana* befalling a particular component leads to the ruin of all other components that must be regarded as more serious.

According to Kautilya the ruler was the most important *prakriti*. Kautilya compares the king to the state as head to the body. If the king is weak the enemy will find it easier to intrigue against the state. The *sastra* also refers to three *saktis* or powers that operate in a state. They are *utsahasakti*, the personal energy and drive of the ruler himself, *prabhavasakti*, the power of the army and the treasury, and *mantraskti*, the power of counsel and diplomacy. These powers are thought of in a state's relations with other states and have no bearing on the internal structure of a state's organisation. Kautilya averred that, for a state's relations with another state *prabhavasakti* is more important than *utsahasakti* and *mantrasakti* is more important than both.

The *Arthaśāstra* also describes the administration of captured territory. Kautilya averred that the *kosha* or treasury is an essential element of the state. A king with a depleted treasury eats into the very vitality of its citizens and the country. At the same time a king who impoverishes his own people or angers them by unjust exactions will lose their loyalty. A balance has thus to be maintained between the welfare of the people and augmenting the resources of the state.

Kautilya also propagates that the prosperity of the state and its inhabitants cannot be maintained unless new territory is acquired by settlement of virgin lands, by alliance or by conquest. In a political environment, which had many states, any state resting content with its own territory was likely to fall prey to the expansionist ambitions of another. A king before moving on a campaign should first ensure that no *vyasana* has befallen any of the constituent elements of the state. The *Arthaśāstra* enumerates the role of state in maintaining the wealth of the nation, in welfare of people, maintaining relation between neighbouring states and conduct of foreign policy based on relative strength of participants. The principles of foreign policy as given out in the *Arthaśāstra* are as applicable today as they were in the third century BC.

Kautilya emphasizes the need of a strong economic and military might for a nation to pursue its national interests and has advocated a foreign policy for achievements of these national interests.

Dandaniti according to Kautilya concerned itself with four things—acquisition of what has not been acquired (*Alabda Labharthah);* preservation of what has been acquired (*Labdh Parirakshana*); augmentation of what has so been preserved; and *Rakshita Vivardhini*, the distribution among the deserving of what has been so augmented. According to Kautilya *Rakshida Vivardhini* is exploitation of natural resources and the development of national income of the country. In today's world any nation will have four instruments of power to pursue its National Interests namely Diplomacy, Information, Military and Economy. The essentials for a strong state are territory, population to include their unity and organisation, military might and economic power. Unity is the constitution of territory and population forming a political unit, and unless the community forms one coherent whole, politically both in its internal and external relations, there can be no state. The organisation in a state presupposes the distinction between the governors and the governed and the establishment of settled relations of control and obedience either given by mutual consent or exacted through compulsion.

Kautilya propounds that any calamity to the people would affect the treasury and thereby the army of the state. For the fort, the treasury and the army all depend on the people. All economic activity according to Kautilya has its source in the population. Kautilya also emphasizes the importance of finance over army.

The army is dependent on a strong finance for its upkeep. Finance is necessary to undertake any state endeavour and is the chief means for both *dharma* (righteous duty) and *kama* (enjoyment). The constituent elements enunciated in the *Arthaśāstra* can be compared to the concept of centre of gravity of a modern state. The strength of a state can be shown by concentric circles representing the following: -

(a) **The Leadership**. The innermost circle is the most important and can be equated with the ruler as enunciated in the *Arthaśāstra*. Weakening of the leadership would lead to the collapse of the state. According to Kautilya any *vyasana* affecting the king would affect all other constituent elements of the state.

(b) **The Industry and Infrastructure**. This forms the economic might of the state. The *Arthaśāstra* mentions it as the *kosa* or the treasury. Any *vyasana* affecting this would affect the population and the military power of the state.

(c) **The Population**. The population is an important element of the centre of gravity of the state. Any *vyasana* befalling the population will have its repercussions on the military capability of the state.

(d) **The Armed Forces**. The armed forces form the outermost ring of the centre of gravity of a state. It protects all other elements of the state from external aggression. But any *vyasana* affecting any other element of the state would have a direct bearing on the armed forces.

For Kautilya the goal set before the ruler is the expansion of the territory. The ruler should be desirous of conquering other territory. Kautilya describes three types of conquerors. *Dharmavijayan*, who makes conquests for the sake of glory, and who is satisfied by mere submission by the other king; *Lobhavijayan*, who makes conquests out of greed and is out to obtain land or money or both; *Asuravijayan,* who makes conquests like a demon and seizes land, money sons and wives of conquered kings and takes his life.

Before starting on an expedition the King should satisfy himself that he is superior in all essential respects to the enemy against whom he proposes to march. A policy of *vigraha* is recommended when one is strong.

The aim of foreign policy of a state is the increase of state's power. This has to be at the cost of the state's enemies or adversaries. Kautilya emphasizes that the state's interests have to be supreme and advocates various policies for the furtherance of these interests.

The means recommended by Kautilya for achievement of national interests are often obnoxious from a moral point of view. Such means are recommended against intractable enemies of the state and are justified in the interests of the state. The morally unjustifiable actions are to be resorted in the supreme interests of the state when the security and independence of the state as such is threatened. Kautilya enumerates that every state considers its own interests as supreme and in their defence resorts to actions that appear unethical.

Kautilya related the defence of a state with its foreign relations. A state has to be defended from its hostile neighbours. Kautilya discusses foreign relations from the point of view of a *vijigisu.* The *vijigisu* is the conqueror state. It seeks to show how a state desirous of extending its influence and expanding its territory, should conduct its relations with other foreign states.

Kautilya sums up the foreign policy in the formula of *sadgunya* or the six measures. It is based on the theory of *Rajamandala* or Circle of Kings. The *mandala* is described to consist of twelve states with *vijigisu* being the conqueror state and the *ari* the hostile state with territory contiguous with the *vijigisu*. In addition are the *madhyama* with territory adjoining that of *vijigisu* and *ari* and stronger than either of these and *udasina*, the state lying outside or the indifferent or neutral king, more powerful than the *vijigisu*, the *ari* and the *madhyama*. Each of these kings would have a *mitra* or ally and *mitramitra* or ally's ally, thus making a total of twelve kings.

This is supported by the common view that two neighbouring states with conflicting interests tend to be hostile to each other and states with common enemy tend to be allies. The *Rajamandala* or *Mandala* as explained by Kautilya was a conglomeration of states loosely divided into two or more less hostile camps with the leader of one group trying to establish its hegemony over the entire conglomeration.

The *Mandala* Concept

The *Mandala* concept is one in which there are circles of friends and foes with the central point being the King and his State. This embraces twelve kings in the vicinity and he considers the kingdoms as neighbours, the states which are the enemies neighbours are his enemies' friends and the next circle of states are his friends. He also believes that the states which are his neighbours and are also neighbours of his enemies are neutral and should always be treated with respect. He believes that this circle is dynamic and the King should strive to be expanding his central position and reduce the power of the other kings in the vicinity. He also proposes to build alliances with states which are two degrees away from the centre to create a balance of power.

The Mandala concept is more multi-polar than the current structure we see. Though our world has emerged into multi-polar on the economic front, it is still uni-polar on the military front. Also the intermediate or middle powers in today's world play a major role. In addition he mentions that war is an outcome of a power struggle and state sovereignty hence he treats diplomacy as a temporary phenomenon. That being said he elaborates on the six forms of diplomacy which are very interesting.

Six Forms of Diplomacy

Kautilya elaborates on strategies for not only the strong king and the aggressor but also explains the strategies a weak king should follow to defend himself and protect the state. His forms of diplomacy also depends on the type of the king whether the policy is directed toward the superior, inferior or equal. The six types of foreign policy that he advocates are

1. *Sandhi*: This means accommodation, which means that kings seek to accommodate the each other and does not resolve to hostile means. These *Sandhis* could be temporary or permanent and it depends on the environment and relative powers of the kings. The various

sub-forms in this *sandhi* have been practiced by statesmen later.

2. *Vigraha*: This means hostility shown to neighbour or a state. Kautilya strongly believed that the states are always at war and seek power hence it is necessary to have hostile foreign policy towards few states which are either equal in power or subordinate in power.
3. *Asana*: This means indifference and he chooses this policy for states which are neutral in his *mandala* concept of nations. He also believes that an indifferent foreign policy works well in the case of equal power. I may not agree on this point as we have seen in case of equal powers in history, there has been always tension which either led to a war or an alliance.
4. *Dvaidhibhava*: This means double policy. Kautilya advocates this foreign policy for states which are superior militarily.
5. *Samsraya*: This policy of protection is followed where a stronger state intervenes and shelters a weak state. Kautilya advocates this policy when a stronger state needs a shield to protect itself from an equal power it is good to use this policy of protection for a third state and use this alliance to defend against the potential enemy.
6. *Yana*: This policy is to attack. Kautilya does mention that peace and stability in a state makes the state even powerful but never shies away from attacking the weak and unjust king. He thinks that an unjust king keeps the society unhappy which makes that state a potential target as it is weak due to social unrest. Kautilya's foreign policy was formed by his strong belief in the King and the state's continuous thirst for power and wealth. His diplomatic tactics were also influenced by Hindu religion and the social structure which shaped his thinking in terms of types of foreign policies and their application.

The Army

Ancient political thinkers of India conceived the state as consisting of seven essential elements of which the army was one, The conception dates from pre-Kautilyan times, and was accepted as an axiomatic truth by all later writers. The army was thus accorded a recognised position in the state-organism. In contemporary thought it usually takes rank as sixth in the order of gradation. There is a discussion in the *Arthaśāstra* as to the relative importance of the army (*danda*) and the treasury (*kosha*), and Kautilya pronounces himself definitely in favour of the latter. "The army", he says, "may go to the enemy, or murder the king himself, and bring about every kind of trouble. But finance is the chief means of observing virtuous acts and of enjoying desires." Later writers, though adhering to the general principles of Kautilya, show a more positive inclination to idolise the army and the relation of the army to the state has been compared with that of the mind to the man. As without the mind the human organism cannot work, so without the army the state-organism comes to a standstill. Without the army there is neither kingdom, nor wealth, nor prowess. The treasury is the root of the army, and the army is the root of the treasury. It is by maintaining the army that the treasury and the kingdom prosper, and the enemy is destroyed.

In the Vedic period the army appears to have consisted of two divisions, viz. foot-soldiers (*patti*) and charioteers (*rathin*) During the post-Vedic period, however the horse and the elephant were incorporated in the fighting corps. This gave rise to the organisation of the army as *chaturanga* or four-fold.

The relative position of the four arms differed from age to age. Initially, the chariots constituted the most important arm. Later, the elephant occupied the first rank in the military service. The infantry and the cavalry seem to have always remained in a subsidiary position in the Hindu military system.

Besides the classification of the army into four arms, there was also in vogue a six-fold division, presumably based on the area or source of recruitment. According to this conception, the army was supposed to consist of six limbs (*sadanga*), these being the hereditary troops (*maula*), mercenaries (*bhrta*), gild levies (*sreni*), soldiers supplied by feudatory chiefs or allies (*surdhbalam*) , troops captured or won over from the enemy (*dvisadbalam*), and forest tribes (*atavibalam*).

Of the different classes of troops the greatest importance was attached to the *maula* or hereditary troops. Graded qualitatively, the mercenaries came next, followed by the gild levies and the allied troops, while the forest tribes were placed at the bottom of the scale. In the *Arthaśāstra*, Kautilya gives elaborate reasons in support of the above gradation. "A *maula* force," he says, "is more important than the *bhrta* force inasmuch as it is dependent on the king for its existence and is the recipient of constant favour from the latter." Mercenaries are better than gild levies because they are obedient to the king, stationed near at hand, and always ready to march. Similarly gild levies are better than allied troops on the ground that they belong to the same country as the king, have the same objects in view, the same expectations of loss and gain, and are actuated by the same feelings of rivalry and anger. Kautilya proceeds in the same strain to show why he considers allied troops superior to renegades from the hostile country; and the latter again to forest tribes. With regard to the last two, he says: "Both are anxious for plunder. In the absence of plunder and in times of difficulty, they prove as dangerous as a lurking snake."

Kautilya speaks of villages which were exempted from taxation in lieu of the military services which they rendered to the state. It seems reasonable to believe that the *maulas* were endowed with rent-free lands, besides cash wages when on active service. Elsewhere, Kautiya outlines the circumstances under which this class of troops should be mobilised against the enemy, "When the king," he writes, "thinks that the number of his *maula* troops is more than is necessary for the defence of his kingdom, or when he apprehends that his *maula* force is disaffected and may cause disturbance when he is away, or when the enemy has under command a large and loyal body of hereditary troops, and is therefore to be fought out with much skill on his part, or when it is expected that the journey would be so tedious and the duration of fight so long that a *maula* force can alone endure the wear and tear, or when the enemy is known to be in possession of a powerful secret service, in which case mercenary and other kinds of troops cannot be relied upon lest they may lend their ears to the intrigues of the enemy, or when the king thinks that other kinds of troops are wanting in strength, then is the time for mobilising the *maula* force. It is thus clear that this class of troops was not only considered as the most reliable, for they alone could be trusted but also possessed the greatest skill and fortitude. And this, in part, accounts for and perhaps justifies the special privileges which the state bestowed upon them.

Two other classes of troops which require some explanation are the gild levies (*sreni*)and the forest tribes(*atavibalam*). They were called *sreni* from an analogy to trade guilds, and, no doubt, served for pay, perhaps under a contract made between the king and the *sreni-mukhya*. This category of soldiers was, perhaps, mustered for a specific operation or campaign. In those times, when there was a weakness of the central government, internecine strife, frequency of brigandage on the highways, which increased the level of insecurity of the population, the industrial and commercial communities fell back on private and local resources to develop a defensive system of their own. This became at once a source of weakness as well as of strength to the state. These levies could rally to support the king on occasions of grave danger to the state; and, if they did not receive their regular wages from the royal exchequer could be a threat, if they were powerful enough to defy the authority of the king. Kautilya did not approve of these gild levies. He asked—which is better, a land with scattered people, or that inhabited by gilds. He preferred the former as it can be kept under control. The gild levies were generally susceptible to the intrigues of the enemy; were intolerant of calamities; and susceptible to anger and other passions. Their distinguishing characteristics were turbulence, truculence and independence.

The mention of *atavibalam* as a part of military establishment in the *Arthaśāstra* shows that the custom of associating predatory hordes with the army goes back to very early times. These predatory hordes used to live in vast forests and inaccessible mountains. They appear have been most numerous in central and peninsular India, though they could also be found in other parts of the country. Both literary and epigraphic evidence prove that they were a constant source of danger to peaceful settlements in their neighbourhood. In the *Arthaśāstra* Kautilya remarks: "Robbers carry off the property of the careless and can be put down as they are easily recognised and caught hold of, whereas wild tribes have their own strongholds, being numerous and brave, ready to fight in broad daylight, and seizing and destroying countries like kings."

Yet these wild tribes were often employed for military purposes by Hindu kings. They brought their own war-apparatus to the theatre of war, but they fought for pay and plunder. Their services were considered especially helpful when a king's army had to pass through forests and defiles, morasses or mountains, or when it was the intention of the invader to ravage and devastate the enemy's country.

It may be noted here that the same custom of associating predatory tribes with the army continued in later ages among the Marathas and the Moghuls. It is well-known that the Pindaris often accompanied a Maratha army in its expeditions, and were employed not so much for fighting as for plundering the country through which they passed. In the Moghul army, along with the troops there marched privileged and recognised thieves who were the first to invade the enemy's territory, where they plundered everything they found. The most bounteous items were reserved for the general; the rest they sold on their own account.

The Infantry

As everywhere else in the world, so in India, the original fighting man was the foot-soldier. In ancient times, the infantry (*patti*) fought along with the chariots. In the A, Kautilya attaches much importance to elephants and even to horses and gives a detailed analysis of the functions of the various arms of the army. But referring to infantry, he simply says that its proper work is to carry weapons to all places and at all times, and drilling. Further elaborating, he says that, "of infantry, cavalry, chariots and elephants, he should strike the first -mentioned with that which is subsequently mentioned," thus clearly indicating his views on the relative efficiency of the different arms.

War Chariots

The use of chariots in warfare marks an important stage in the evolution of the world's military system. Man was, as stated before, originally a foot-soldier. But when tribes were fused into states, and distant marches became a necessity, it must have been found that a foot-soldier who, encumbered with arms and armour, had a long distance to march before coming to close quarters with his adversary, was at the disadvantage at the commencement of the conflict. It was then realised that the soldier who could be carried without fatigue and be fresh to exert every energy in deadly conflict, would have a great advantage in a hand-to-hand struggle over one who had been obliged to march heavily laden for a long distance. This is probably one of the most important reasons which led to the use of chariots in ancient warfare. But there was possibly another equally important reason The chariot-warrior could carry with him a larger number of weapons than an ordinary foot-soldier. Moreover, being elevated over his opponent, and partly protected from his weapons by the chariot-screen, he enjoyed an advantage over a foot soldier. The use of war-chariots was not an isolated phenomenon in the history of India.

In the *Arthaśāstra,* Kautilya described the different kinds of chariots used both for peaceful and warlike purposes. Of the latter, he especially specifies three, viz. the *sangramika* (battle chariots), the *parapurabhiyanika* (chariots used in assaulting the enemy's strongholds), and the *vainayika* (training chariots). Regarding the size of chariots, he mentions that the best chariots should accommodate ten persons, and in extreme cases twelve. After this there should be six more varieties of chariots with gradually decreasing weight and size till we come down to one which might contain four persons ordinarily, and six in exceptional cases.

Cavalry

It is difficult to fix the period at which cavalry, in the proper sense of the word, were first used in India. Nevertheless, it must be noted that that the cavalry never came to occupy the front rank in the army organisation of ancient India and never became the core of the armies. One of the reasons why there could not evolve a strong cavalry system in ancient India, comparable in strength and efficiency to that of the Greeks, or later the Muhammadans, was the lack of good horses in India.

The gradual emergence of the cavalry as an efficient arm is attested by the nature and variety of functions assigned to them in the *Arthaśāstra*. Kautilya mentions that "running against ;running round ; running beyond; running back; disturbing the enemy's halt; gathering the troops; curving, circling, miscellaneous operations; removal of the rear, pursuit of the line from the front, flanks and rear; protection of the broken army; and falling upon the broken army—these are the forms of waging war with the horses. He defines the principal tasks of the cavalry as consisting in cutting off the provisions and reinforcements of the enemy, screening and protecting the strategic front of the armies, outpost and detached service, occupying advanced positions, delivering a charge, scouting and reconnoitring, gaining the flanks and rear of an enemy, covering an advance and pursuing a retreating foe. In other words, they were expected to intervene in the prologue, in the principal act, and in the dénouement.

Kautilya also contemplates an array of pure cavalry in which the centre is to be occupied by heavy armoured horsemen, and the flanks and wings by those without armour. The lack of horse-archers was a fatal lack in the military system of ancient India. The *Arthaśāstra* however, provides a detailed account of the various movements employed for the training of horses. There were five principal movements of horses—circular, slow, jumping, gallop and movement following signals. These, again, consisted of several varieties.

Elephants

Once elephants were tamed and domesticated, it did not take long to realise their extraordinary strength could be used profitably for military purposes. In succeeding centuries, the importance of elephants went on mounting higher and higher in Indian military estimation. Kautilya provides us with inkling into the military thought of his age when he writes that "it is on elephants that the destruction of an enemy's army depends." "The victory of kings in battles", he remarks elsewhere "depends mainly upon elephants for elephants; being of large bodily frame, are able not only to destroy the arrayed army of enemy, his fortifications and encampments, but also to undertake works that are dangerous to life.

Most ancient politico-military writers have attempted to formulate the functions which a trained elephant corps was expected to perform in war. According to Kautilya, the most important of these functions were:

(a) acting as the vanguard of a marching army (*puroyanam*)

(b) preparing roads, camping grounds and landing ghats in rivers (*akrtamarga-vasa-tirtha-karma*)

(c) clearing away such impediments as small trees and shrubs (*visama-sambadha-pravesa*)

(d) battering down walls, gates and towers of a fortress (*saladvarattalaka-bhanjanam*) and

(e) breaking up, scattering or trampling down the hostile force.

The training of elephants for war would have involved a more laborious process than the training of horses. According to the *Arthaśāstra*, the training of elephants consisted of several clearly marked stages. The process began when the animal was brought to attach itself to a herd of tamed elephants, and lost its wildness by contact with them; this was called the *yuthagata* stage of training. Then the animal was cleverly thrown into a pit specially dug to subdue its ferocity; this was the *apapata* stage. The next step in the training (*varigata*) was to keep the animal confined within a particular area of the forest instead of allowing if to roam at large. The next disciplinary measure was to tie the animal to a post when it was found to be sufficiently gentle for the purpose (*stambhagata*). The taming was completed when the animal became so gentle that it allowed its driver or trainer to sit on its withers without protest; this was the *skandhagata* stage.

When sufficiently tamed, elephants were divided into two groups, viz., those meant for peaceful traffic and those for warlike services. According to Kautilya, the military training of elephants comprised two successive stages. In the first, they were accustomed to girths (*kaksyakarma*), collars (*graiveyakarma*), and to cooperation with a herd of trained elephants in a joint work (*yuthakarma*). In the second, they were trained in the following manoeuvres:

(a) *upasthana* (drill, such as riding, bending, jumping over fences, ropes etc.)

(b) *samvartana* (lying down, sitting and leaping over pits and lines drawn)

(c) *samyana* (moving forward straight or transverse, or making serpentine movements)

(d) *vadhdvadha* (trampling down and killing)

(e) *hastiyuddha* (fighting with other elephants)

(f) *nagarayana* (assailing forts and cities) and

(g) *samgramika* (other cognate movements relating to war)

Naval Warfare

There are reasons for thinking that naval warfare though not widely practised, was not unknown in ancient India. Ancient writers sometimes speak of fighting galleys as constituting a part of the royal military establishment. In the *Arthaśāstra* , while describing the functions of the Superintendent of Ships (*navadhyaksa*), Kautilya remarks: "Pirate ships (*himsrika*), boats from an enemy's country when they cross its territorial limits; as well as vessels violating the customs and rules enforced in port towns, should be pursued and destroyed." It is obvious that the task set forth above could only be performed by armed vessels belonging to the state.

Military Espionage

Spies filled an important role in both, civil and military affairs, in ancient India. The *Arthaśāstra* provides us with a graphic account of the activities of spies in the Mauryan polity. Spies, were primarily divided into two classes viz. local agents (*samsthah*) wandering or travelling supervisors (*samcarah*).To the former category belonged spies under the guise of a 'fraudulent disciple' (*kapatika-chatra*), recluse (*udasthita*), householder (*grahapatika*) merchant (*vaidehaka*), and ascetic practising austerities (*tapasa*); while under the latter group came spies called classmate (*satri*), firebrand' (*tiksna*), poisoner (*rasada*), and mendicant woman (*bhiksuki*). The mention of monks, ascetics and mendicant women as spies provides an eloquent commentary on Kautilya's religious attitude. Though a Brahman, and certainly a believer in the established order of society, he had no hesitation in advocating an unscrupulous exploitation of the religious susceptibilities of the people. But the spies were to put on an unlimited variety of disguises. Moreover, as far as practicable, they were not to be known to each other; and the king must, on no account, rely upon the report of a single spy. There were Institutes of Espionage, controlling the entire intelligence department, and checking and verifying the reports coming from different sources. Cipher writing was used by the spies, and carrier pigeons carried secret intelligence.

There were numerous duties which the spies had to perform. They were to watch the conduct of government officials of all ranks, from the highest to the lowest. They were to keep the king informed about the trend of public feeling in the kingdom. They were to detect sedition and crime, and assist in the administration of justice. Last but not least, they had to collect accurate information regarding the state of affairs in neighbouring kingdoms, discover and foil the ruses of the other side and neutralise its successes.

Broadly speaking, in relation to foreign states espionage took three forms, viz., political, diplomatic and military. The first involved an attempt to get into touch through secret emissaries with the discontented or disloyal elements in the hostile state, and utilize their services for the destruction of the latter. Various forms of political espionage of this kind have been elaborated by Kautilya.

Diplomatic espionage was carried on by ambassadors and diplomatic agents in foreign courts. The duties of these officers in peacetime included not merely the carrying out of negotiations but also observation of what went on in the kingdoms to which they were accredited. They were specially expected to keep an eye on all matters which, directly or indirectly, affected the interests of the state they represented. While discussing the duties of the ambassador (*duta*), Kautilya lays down: "The envoy shall make friendship with the enemy's officers such as those in charge of wild tracts, of boundaries, of cities, and of country parts. He shall also contrast the military stations, sinews of war, and strongholds of the enemy with those of his own master. He shall ascertain the size and area of forts and of the state, as well as strong-holds of precious things, and assailable and unassailable points." Further, "he shall through the agency of ascetic and merchant spies or through his disciples or through spies under the guise of physicians and heretics or through the recipients of salaries from two states (*ubhayavetana*) ascertain the nature of the intrigue prevalent among parties favourably disposed to his own master, as well as the conspiracy of hostile factions, and understand the loyalty or disloyalty of the people to the enemy, besides any assailable points. If there is no possibility of carrying on such conversation, he may try to gather such information by observing the talk of beggars, intoxicated and insane persons, or of persons babbling in sleep, or by observing the signs made in places of pilgrimage and temples, or by deciphering paintings and secret writings (*citra-gudha-lekhya-samjnabhih*). It is thus clear that an ambassador in ancient India, like his modern prototype, was nothing more than an honourable spy acting under the protection of the customary law.

Military espionage consisted in the employment of secret agents to procure accurate information regarding the military resources of the hostile state. plans and movements of the hostile army, and safeguarding one's own camp and army from the poisonous contamination of enemy's spies. Kautilya speaks or "spies who are residing as traders in the enemy's forts, and those that are living as cultivators in the enemy's villages, as well as those who are living as cowherds or ascetics in the district borders of the enemy's country." Further, Kautilya advocates the employment of spies along with the marching army in the camp, and also in the fighting line. They were to keep up the morale of the troops by declaring the success of their operations and the failure of those of the enemy. They were also to harass the enemy, create divisions in their ranks, and demoralise the hostile king by telling him that his own fort was burnt, stormed or that someone of his family or an enemy or wild chief rose in rebellion. In the work of espionage all methods were admissible -spying, lying, bribing, poisoning, woman's wiles and the assassin's knife.

To a weak king, menaced by a strong neighbour, Kautilya's advice is to rely chiefly on spies, and wage what he describes as 'battle of intrigue' (*mantra-yuddha*) and 'secret war' (*kuta-yuddha*). The spies were to practise all kinds of fraud, artifice, incendiarism and robbery. They were to demoralise the enemy's troops by circulating false news, and seduce the allegiance of his ministers and commanders. The underlying idea seems to have been to keep the strong neighbour so preoccupied with domestic troubles as to make it impossible for him to launch upon a foreign expedition.

In capturing a fort, Kautilya advises the invading king to infuse enthusiastic spirit among his own men and frighten the enemy's people by giving publicity to his power of omniscience and close association with gods. The circulation of this precious information was to be entrusted to spies disguised as "astrologers, soothsayers, horologists, storytellers (*pauranika*), as well as those who read the forebodings of every moment. To induce credence in the story, the spies were to perform certain religious and magical tricks such as the shower of firebrand (*ulka*) with the noise of drums (from the sky) on the day of the birth-star of the enemy. They were also to spread rumours about the justice and magnanimity of the invading king. When the people of the enemy were convinced of this, they may be sent to the conqueror to receive wealth and honour. Those of the enemy who were in need of money and food should be supplied with an abundance of those things. Those who do not like to receive such things may he presented with ornaments for their wives and children. By methods such as these, the invading king was to create a party favourable to his interests in the enemy's fort, and later to capture it through their help.

Recruitment

The lower classes of society—the *Vaisyas* and *Sudras*—were not excluded from military service. The truth, on the contrary, seems to be that they constituted the rank and file of the army, in spite of the formal law that men might follow the profession of a lower caste, if unable to sustain themselves by what appertained to their own, but must never follow the profession of a higher caste. Casteless forest tribes were often employed by Hindu kings for military purposes. They fought when necessity called them into the field. Kautilya approved of the employment of *Vaisya* and *Sudra* troops in the army.

Military Organisation

In the *Arthaśāstra*, Kautilya mentions that for every ten members of each of the constituents of the army, there must be one commander, called *padika*; ten *padikas* under a *senapati* ; ten *senapatis* under a *nayaka*. Thus according to Kautilya, the smallest unit of the army was a squad of ten, which was commanded by a *padika*. Ten such squads formed a platoon of a hundred, officered by a *senapati*. Ten platoons constituted a regiment under the command of a general, called *nayaka*.

Training of the Army

The importance of exercise, drill and training for the army was recognised from early times. Kautilya states that it is possible to infuse spirit and enthusiasm, even in timid troops, by means of discipline and training. He further states: "Footmen, horses, chariots and elephants shall be given necessary training in the art of war at sunrise on all days but those of conjunction of the planets; on these occasions of training, the king shall ever be present and witness the exercise."

Kautilya also says: "The *nayaka* will, by means of trumpet sounds, flags and ensigns (*turyaghosa-patakabhih*), signal to the constituents of his army as to when they are to form into divisions (*anga-vibhae*), when to unite into a compact body (*samghate*), when to halt (*sthane*), when to turn back from the combat and when to make onslaughts." It is only logical to conclude that troops were trained in times of peace in the technique of movements according to signs and sounds.

Pay and Emoluments, Rewards and Honours

Most ancient writers strongly emphasise the necessity of making regular payment to troops. In the *Arthaśāstra* Kautilya considers the withholding of soldiers' pay as one of the primary causes that breed discontent and trouble in the army. There is also a chapter in the *Arthaśāstra* which dwells on the salaries to be given to different categories of officials of the state. It is clear that the scale of pay was fairly high. The following details regarding the salaries and wages of commanders, corporals, troops and servants in the military establishment are available:

	Officer	**Salary per annum**
(a)	Commander-in-chief	48,000 *panas*
(b)	*Nayaka*	12,000 *panas*
(c)	Officers-in-charge of elephants, horses, chariots and infantry and heads of guilds (*srenimukhya*)	8,000 *panas*
(d)	Superintendents (*adhyaksas*) of infantry, cavalry, chariots and elephants	4,000 *panas*
(e)	Physician of the army, chariot driver (*rathika*), horse and elephant trainer	2,000 *panas*
(f)	Superintendent of the armoury	1,000 *panas*
(g)	Trained soldiers	500 *panas*
(h)	Trumpet-blowers (*turyakara*)	500 *panas*
(i)	Elephant mahout (according to efficiency)	500-1,000 *panas*
(j)	Stationary (*samsthah*) spies	1,000 *panas*
(k)	Wandering (*sancarah*) spies	500 *panas*
(l)	Servants leading the spies (in proportion to work done)	200 *panas*

It is also of interest that the scales of pay for both the civil and military officers of the state, as given in the *Arthaśāstra*., suggest an extensive and prosperous empire. Another point which calls for attention is that Kautilya allots a salary of 4,000 *panas* to the superintendents of infantry, cavalry, chariots and elephants; but he assigns only 1,000 *panas* as the salary of other departmental heads (*adhyaksas*). It is logical to conclude that in the age of Kautilya's the state attached much greater importance to the army than to its civil departments,

Besides salaries ant} wages in cash, officers and soldiers in the army were sometimes rewarded with exemptions from land-revenue, sometimes with assignments of land. Kautilya also mentions that villages were exempted from taxation in lieu of the military services which they rendered to the state. Elsewhere in the *Arthaśāstra*, while describing the methods and measures for colonisation of lands, Kautilya says: "Superintendents, accountants, *gopas*, *sthanikas*, veterinary surgeons, physicians, horse-trainers, and messengers shall be endowed with lands, which they shall have no right to alienate by sale or mortgage. In another context, however, he remarks that a king, who wants to maintain some uniformity of standard throughout his kingdom, must on no account endow his officers and servants with villages.

Besides pay, either in the shape or salaries or land assignments, officers and troops were, occasionally, given special allowances on the eve of an expedition. Soldiers who displayed special courage in the course of a battle were sometimes rewarded with an increase in their pay and rations, sometimes with special monetary allotments, and, in the case of officers, by promotion in rank and honour. In the *Arthaśāstra* there is described a graded list of monetary rewards to be given to troops for acts of special merit. A hundred thousand *panas* for slaying the enemy king; fifty thousand for slaying the commander-in-chief and the heir-apparent; ten thousand for slaying the chief of the brave; five thousand for destroying an elephant or a chariot; a thousand for killing a horse, a hundred *panas* for slaying the chief of the infantry; twenty for bringing a head; and twice the pay in addition to whatever is seized.

Kautilya also mentions that the wives of soldiers slain on duty should be provided for with subsistence and wages. Infants, aged persons or diseased persons related to the deceased shall also be shown favour. He also mentions that, on occasions of funerals, sickness, or child-birth, the king shall give presents to his servants concerned therein.

Having a well-paid, organised, and highly motivated standing army and the economic wealth needed to raise a territorial army along with local militias and auxiliaries were but one component of warfare. Kautilya, like Clausewitz, regarded war as a means to an end—or an extension of policy though the application of force. And, like Sun Tzu, Kautilya regarded the period before the actual fighting began as critical to the outcome. It was vital that the ruler and his servants be able and willing to undertake a dispassionate and rational appreciation of the total assets of their state in relation to the enemy (or enemies) modified by the contributions of allies. Thus, geography, timing, seasonal variations, mobilisation schedules, preparing for internal rebellions and discontent, estimating the material losses in relation to strategic gains, and the risks involved to the stability of the dynasty all had to be carefully weighed. There was no point in attacking a more powerful state without first consulting one's allies. Similarly, committing troops to a limited engagement without factoring the possibility of escalation and the likely losses was to be avoided. While the military was trained and drilled into believing in itself and the power of positive thinking, for the ruler and his senior servants, optimism was a dangerous and potentially catastrophic luxury. Indeed, for Kautilya the power of solid advice was greater than military strength, and by combining superior intelligence and comprehension of politics the conqueror could prevail against militarily more powerful adversaries.

Combat

Kautilya mentions that favourable positions for infantry, cavalry, chariots and elephants are desirable both for war and the camp. For men who are trained to fight in desert tracts, forests, valleys, or plains, and for those who are trained to fight from ditches or heights; during the day or night, and for elephants which are bred in countries with rivers, mountains, marshes or lakes as well as for horses, such battle-fields as they should find suitable are to be selected. It is evident that, according to Kautilya, the primary consideration which should weigh with a general in selecting a position must be the character and composition of his forces. It was universally recognised that the different arms required different grounds for the proper discharge of their functions. A commander was expected to keep this fact persistently in view, and dispose troops in harmony with the ground on which they were to act.

Highlighting the importance of time and place, Kautilya mentions that: "In daytime the crow kills the owl. At night the owl kills the crow. Thus the time of fight is important. Similarly, "A dog on land drags a crocodile; and a crocodile in water drags a dog." to emphasize that the place of fight is important.

In another context, Kautilya says: "That part of the country in which his army finds a convenient place for its manoeuvres and which proves unfavourable to his foe is the best; that part of the country which is of the reverse nature is the worst; and that which partakes of both the characteristics is a country of middling quality". In other words, the amount of advantage which a position offers to the belligerent was to be the sole criterion of its merit or demerit, A general in command must have the military insight to recognise whether a particular position would be advantageous for the manoeuvre of his troops.

In describing battle orders or formations, Kautilya broadly speaking divides them under four main heads, viz. *danda* (staff), *bhoga* (snake), *mandala* (circle) and *asamhata* (detached order). Each of these, again, is subdivided into several varieties. Thus the *danda* comprised seventeen, the *bhoga* five, the *mandala* two, and the *asamhata* six varieties of arrays or formations. Apart from these, there were various other arrays known.

The *danda* (staff) as an array in which the troops in the different divisions were deployed in curved lines or columns has been described by Kautilya as a battle-order in which the wings, flanks and vanguard of the army were maintained in equal strength. The seventeen varieties of this order were: *dandavyuha* called *pradara* (breaking the enemy's army) when its flanks are made to project in front. It is, again, known as *drdhaka* (firm) when its wings are stretched back. It is called *asahya* (irresistible) when its wings are stretched forward towards the enemy. When after the formation of the wings, the front is made to bulge outwards it is called *syena* (hawk). These four varieties are called *capa* (bow), *capakuksi* (the centre of the bow), *pratistha* (hold) and *suprathistha* (stronghold) respectively when they are arranged in the reverse order.

That variety of the *dandavyuha* in which the wings are arranged in the shape of a bow was called *sanjaya* (victory). The same with a projected front was called *vijaya*. The array which had its wings drawn up in the shape of a flat ear was called *sthulakarna*, the array in which the wings are made twice as flat as those of a *vijaya* was known as *visala-vijaya* (great victory); that in which the flanks and the vanguard were stretched towards the wings was called *camumukha* ; and the same was called *jhasahya* when it is arrayed in the reverse form. That variety of *danda* in which the troops were made to stand one behind another, was called *suimukha* (needle-faced) array. When the array consists of two such lines, it was called *valaya*; and when of four lines, it was called *durjaya* (invincible).

According to Kautilya the chief distinctive feature of the *bhoga* battle formation was the fact that its wings, flanks and front were of unequal depth. The five varieties of this order were: *sarpasari* (which had a serpentine movement), *gomutrika* (course of a cow's urine), *sakata* (wagon), *makara* (crocodile) and *paripatantaka*. Some of these have been defined. Thus the wagon was explained as that variety of *bhoga* in which the front is divided into two parts, and the wings are arranged in the form of staffs. The reverse of this was described as the crocodile array. The *paripatantaka*, again, was said to have been a variety of the wagon, having in its columns a large number of elephants, horses and chariots.

The *mandala* (circular array) has been defined as a battle order in which the wings, flanks and front stood in close proximity to one another, without having any intermediate space between them. Its two varieties were known as *sarvatobhadra* and *durjaya*. When the battle-order was so arranged as to face in all directions, it was called *sarvatobhadra*. When, again, though having the flanks as usual, its front was split up into two halves and the wings into four, it was termed *durjaya*.

The *asamhata* was explained as an array in which the wings, flanks and front were stationed apart from each other. The six varieties of this order were known as the thunderbolt (*vajra*), alligator (*godha*), park (*udyanaka*), crow-footed (*kakapadi*), crescent (*ardha-candrika*), and *karkata-srngi*. Besides these, battle-orders were formed in various other ways. Kautilya writes that "the array in which the chariots form the front, the elephants the wings, and horses the rear, is called *arista*; that in which infantry, cavalry, chariots and elephants stand one behind the other is called *acala*; that in which elephants, horses, chariots and infantry stand in order one behind the other is known as *apratihata*." When, again, the wings were occupied by elephants, the flanks by horses, and the front by chariots, it was called a *cakra* (wheel) array. When the front was occupied by elephants, the flanks by chariots and the wings by horses it was known as a *madhya-bhedi* array. There was also what has been described as an *antarbhedi* array. In this the flanks were occupied by elephants, the wings by chariots and the front by cavalry. It is needless to expand the list further.

From the foregoing enumeration it is clear that the disposition of troops on the battlefield could in fact take any form or shape. The nature of the formation adopted by a general on any particular occasion was determined by various considerations. In the first place, is the composition of the forces at his disposal. The second determining factor was the character of the theatre of operations. Kautilya says that: "nature of the ground in the front or on the sides or in the rear should be examined. On an even site the *danda*, and the *mandala* array should be formed; on an uneven ground *bhoga* and *asamhata* arrays should be made; and on a site of a complex nature, the battle-order should be of the *visama* type. The ruler should devise one, two or more of these *vyuha* or a mixture of them according to the number of troops and the character of roads and battle-fields". The third factor which decided the nature of the array was the strength and character of the enemy's battle-array. Kautilya averred that one should assail the *pradara* by means of the *capa*, *pratistha* by means of the *supratistha*, *sanjaya* by means of the *vijaya*, *sthulakarna* by means of the *visala-vijaya*, and *paripatantaka* by means of the *sarvato-bhadra*. One may assail all kinds of arrays by means of the *durjaya*. It was enjoined that a large force, fighting against a small one, should be arrayed in extended lines, but a small force, in order to compete with a large one, should charge in one long narrow column, concentrating all its strength at one point.

Besides the formation of battle-arrays, there are few other details regarding the disposition of the army on the field of battle. In the *Arthaśāstra* it is stated that foot-soldiers should be so arrayed that the space between any two men might be equivalent to one *sama* (fourteen finger-widths); horses should be arrayed with three *samas* as the intervening space; while chariots and elephants should be stationed five *samas* apart. In more extended arrays, however, the intervening space between any two individuals could be doubled or trebled. When the army consisted of a large contingent of archers, the rules appear to have been slightly different. The space intervening between any two bowmen was to be equivalent to a *dhanus* (five times the length of the forearm), that between horses fifteen cubits, and that between chariots and war-elephants twenty-five cubits. This increase in space was probably necessitated by the fact that archers required more room for the effective use of their weapons. With regard to the different divisions of an array, Kautilya holds that in ordinary circumstances they should he ranged twenty-five cubits apart from each other.

Qualitatively, troops were considered as falling under four classes: viz. *saram* (best), *anusaram* (second best), *trtiyasaram* (third in rank), and *phalgu* (weak troops). Kautilya laid down that in drawing up a formation the general should place the weaker troops (*phalgu*) in the forefront of each division. Then should be deployed the *trtiyasaram*, and then the best. The second best (*anusaram*) is to be placed in the rear line. The reason offered for this arrangement is typically illustrative of the intensely practical nature of Kautilyan military precepts. If the weakest troops be placed in the front line, he argued, the first shock of the enemy charge would fall upon them, and not a single soldier of the better type would perish. When the enemy is thus engaged in an encounter with the riff-raff of the army (*phalgu-bala*), the general should manoeuvre his best troops, swoop down upon the enemy and annihilate him. Elsewhere, however, he recommended that the best troops should be placed in the vanguard, and the weaker troops in the rear.

Battle Tactics

It may appear that, while much ingenuity was expended on the formation of battle-arrays, it did not have a decisive influence on the conduct of battles. A general impression is that, after the first engagement, there was little order maintained on the battlefield and that it was a combat of duels and push. However, in the *Arthaśāstra* a clear enunciation of some fundamental principles of tactics is mentioned, which perhaps shows that commanders of armies followed some definite plan in conducting a campaign. For instance, it is laid down that when an army is drawn up in battle-order, the general must not move it *en masse* against the enemy but should rather assail the latter with one or two divisions, and when the enemy is thrown into confusion, should follow up the first onset with the remaining divisions. A second principle enunciated is that a commander must begin a battle by striking that portion of the hostile army which is occupied by weak and treacherous troops. Thirdly, it is emphasised that he should make a rear-attack on the enemy, when a frontal attack is considered disadvantageous, and a, frontal attack under contrary circumstances. Similarly when an attack on one wing or flank is deemed unwise, the other wing or flank may be assailed. Having struck the front of the hostile army, the commander should follow it up by an attack from the rear. He may also strike at the enemy's rear, and then when it has wheeled round, must attack it from the front. Finally, it lay down that a commander must not press hard a weak but desperate foe, secure in a strong position; for "when a broken army, reckless of life, resumes its attack, its fury becomes irresistible."

This necessity of addressing encouraging words to the troops on the eve of a conflict is also emphasised in the *Arthaśāstra* . Kautilya wrote that: "A virtuous king should call his army together, and, specifying the place and time of battle, address them thus: I am a paid servant like yourselves; this country is to be enjoyed (by me) together with you; you have to strike the enemy specified by me," The minister and priest of the king should also similarly exhort the army. They should say: "It is declared in the Vedas that the goal which is reached by sacrifices, after performing the final ablutions, in sacrifices in which the priests have been duly paid for, it is the very goal which brave men are destined to attain." It is further enjoined that bards and astrologers in the king's entourage should point out to the troops the impregnable nature of their array, belittle the strength of the enemy, and assert that, owing to their association with the gods and their knowledge of the auguries, they were convinced that the king was sure to win the day. Soothsayers (*sutah*) and court bards (*magadhah*) should humour the troops by extolling their caste, community, family, past deeds and character, and the followers of the priest should loudly proclaim that sacrifices were being performed for the complete annihilation of the enemy.

Kautilya also remarks that: "physicians with surgical instruments and appliances and healing ointments and bandages, and women with food and drink should stand behind encouraging the fighting men". He enjoins that the king should have in his camp not merely a rich store of medicine, but also expert physicians equipped with surgical instruments (*sarvo-pakaranair-yuktan vaidyamsca suvisaradan*). It shows that provision of medical aid to sick and wounded troops was regarded as an important duty of the state. But to what extent such aid was actually provided, how it was organised, how far it was effective are questions on which no light is thrown.

Fortifications

Nowhere perhaps are the ancient Hindu ideas on fortification better delineated than in the *Arthaśāstra* of Kautilya. In common with his predecessors in the field of political speculation, Kautilya considered the fort as one of the seven constituent elements of the state. Doubtless it was not the most important, but it was more important than the treasury, the friend and the army itself. "For it is in the fort that the treasury and the army are safely kept, and it is from the fort that secret war (intrigue), control over one's partisans, the upkeep of the army, the reception of allies and the driving out of enemies are successfully practised. In the absence of forts, the treasury is to the enemy, for it seems that for those who own forts, there is no destruction." Elsewhere he says that "the haven of the king and of his army is a strong fort."

With these preliminary remarks about the importance of fortifications, Kautilya goes on to classify forts on the basis of their location. In his view, forts might be classified under four principal heads, viz. *parvata* (hill fort), *audaka* (water fort), *dhanvana* (desert fort) and *vanadurga* (forest fort). He defines a hill fort as one which is either perched on a rocky precipice (*prastaram*) or built in a valley in the midst of an encircling range of hills (*guha*). A water fort, he says, may be situated on an island in the midst of a river (*antardvipam*), or on a plain surrounded by low ground or swamps in which water is stagnated (*nimnavaruddham sthalam*). Similarly a forest fort is either encompassed by marshes, interspersed with trees and bushes (*khajanodakam*), or surrounded by thickly-set tall trees with undergrowth (*stambagaham*). Finally, a desert fort is one which is located either in the centre of a wild tract devoid of water or even of thickets (*nirudaka-stambam*), or in a region sterilised by desert salt (*irina*).

Of these different varieties, Kautilya gives his preference to hill-forts and considers them as the most unassailable. He says: "Of forts such as a fort on the plain, in the centre of a river and on a mountain, that which is mentioned later is of more advantage than the one previously mentioned." In an earlier chapter he explains the reasons which led him to this view. "Of two fortified kings," he says, "one who has his forts on a plain is more easily reduced than the other owning a fort in the centre of a river, for a fort in a plain can be easily assailed, destroyed or captured along with the enemy in it, whereas a fort surrounded by a river requires twice as much effort to capture, and supplies the enemy with water and other necessaries of life."

Again: "Of two kings, one owning a fort surrounded by a river and another having mountainous. fortifications, seizing the former's land is better, for a fort in the centre of a river can be assailed by a bridge formed of elephants made to stand in a row in the river, or by wooden bridges, or by means of boats; and the river will not always be deep and can be emptied of its water, whereas a fort on a mountain is of a self-defensive nature, and not easy to besiege or to ascend; and where if one portion of the army defending it is routed out, the other portions can escape unhurt, and such a fort is of immense service, as it affords facilities to throw down heaps of stone and trees over the enemy."

With this estimate of the relative value of forts, Kautilya asks the ruler to create defensive works "on all the four quarters of the boundaries of the kingdom, on grounds naturally best fitted for the purpose. But apart from these, the king must have in the centre of his kingdom, in a locality naturally best fitted for the purpose, such as the bank or the confluence of rivers; a deep pool of perennial water, or of a lake or tank,-a fortified capital. This might be of any shape, circular, rectangular or square, in consonance with the requirements of the ground. It has to be surrounded by three successive ditches, the first 84 feet (14 *dandas*), the second 72 feet (12 *dandas*) and the third 60 feet (10 *dandas*) wide, with depth less by one-quarter or one-half of their width." The sides of the ditches were to be built of stones or bricks and they were to be filled with perennial flowing water drawn from some neighbouring river. Crocodiles and lotus plants were to be nurtured in the ditches so that no enemy could swim across them with impunity.

At a distance of 24 feet from the inner-moat ditch, a rampart (*vapra*) 86 feet high and twice as broad, is to be erected "by heaping mud upwards and by making it square at the bottom, oval at the centre, pressed by the trampling of elephants and bulls."Gaps in the rampart must be filled up with fresh earth. The intervening space between the rampart and the ditch is to be strewn with thorny bushes, sharp instruments and entanglements of various kinds.

"Above the rampart are to be erected walls or parapets (*prakara*) built of brick. They might be of any number, with a space of 12 to 24 cubits between them; and they should be twice as high as they are broad. The parapets are to be interspersed at regular intervals with towers or bastions (*attalaka*), square throughout and provided with movable staircases. In the intermediate space measuring 30 *dandas* between two towers, there shall be formed a broad street in two compartments covered with a roof and two and a half times as long as it is broad. This street appears to have been intended for patrol of the sentinels, protected overhead by the roofs. The bifurcation of the street is for facilitating double movements, forward and backward, of the guards on duty. "Between the tower and the broad street, shall be constructed an *indrakosa*, which is made up by covering pieces of perforated wooden planks affording seats for three archers." The entrance gate to the fort should be one-sixth as broad as the width of the street, and above the gateway should be constructed a turret, its face resembling a large lizard. Besides the main gate, there must also be special secret passages for flight or exit in an unassailable part of the rampart.

In addition, Kautilya gives other details regarding the construction of roads and buildings within the fort. He also writes of the construction of canals (*kulya*) to hold weapons. "In these canals, there shall be collected stones, spades (*kuddala*) axes (*kuthari*), varieties of staffs, cudgels (*musranthi*) , hammers (*mudgara*), clubs, discus, machines (*yantra*), and such weapon as can destroy a hundred persons at once (*sataghni*), together with spears, tridents, bamboo-sticks with pointed edges made of iron, camel-necks, explosives (*agni-samyoga*) and whatever else can be devised and formed from available materials." In the chapter on the Superintendent of Armoury he gives a list of various immovable machines (*sthira-yantra*), which were to be specially stored in forts to repulse assaults upon them. He further recommends that articles of food, fodder and fuel should be stored in the fort in such quantities as can be enjoyed for years together. Of such collections, he emphasizes, old items should be replaced once new ones are received.

Siege-craft

In the *Arthaśāstra*, while describing the various devices by which an enemy fort could be captured, Kautilya remarks that a besieging king "may assail the rampart and parapets by making use of underground tunnels and iron rods.'" But it does not seem that mining ever came into general vogue. It is probable that as most of the Indian fortresses were built on high ground or upon a foundation of solid rock, mining was considered entirely useless as a tool of siege-craft: But the word *surunga* with its military implication continued to be known, and ultimately passed over into Hindi vocabulary.

The use of fire, too, for the reduction of a fortified place was not unknown. On this Kautilya supplies us with the following account: "Having captured the birds, such as vulture, crow, parrot, *maina* and pigeon, which have their nests in the fort walls, and having tied to their tails inflammable powder (*agniyoga*), he may let them fly to the forts. If the camp is situated at a distance from the fort and is provided with an elevated post for archers and their flags, then the enemy's fort may be set on fire. Spies, living as watchmen of the fort, may tie inflammable powder to the tails of mongooses, monkeys, cats and dogs and let them go over the thatched roofs of the houses. A splinter of fire kept in the body of a dried fish may be caused to be carried off by a monkey, or a crow, or any other bird, to the thatched roofs of the houses."

He further describes the ingredients of various inflammable compounds which might be prepared and utilised for setting fire to an enemy fort. But he concludes with the following salutary advice: "When a fort can be captured by other means, no attempt should be made to set fire to it; for fire cannot be trusted; it not only offends gods, but also destroys the people, grains, cattle, gold, raw materials and the like. Also, the acquisition of a fort, with its property all destroyed, is a source of further loss." His advice, however, did not always restrain belligerents from resorting to this infamous method.

But the most usual method employed to get over the resistance of a fortress was by investment and starving it out. The besiegers tried to cut off the besieged from communication with the outside world and thus to prevent them from receiving reinforcements or supplies and to make them dependent upon such stores as they may have been able to lay in beforehand, or might be able to produce within the town. The methods of repelling a siege or assault must have varied. According to Kautilya, all possible impediments were to be placed before the enemy to prevent a close investment. Grass and firewood round the fortress were to be set on fire and destroyed as far as a *yojana* (five and half miles); all water channels or pools were also to be either destroyed or vitiated; and a system of secret wells, hidden pits and barbed iron cords should be devised all around the fort.

As against mining, the best device which the besieged could employ was to countermine, and then attack the diggers below ground; drive them back, and fill up the hole they had excavated. The term for the countermine was *prati-sururanga*. The *Arthaśāstra* describes how and when it was to be constructed: "When the enemy attempts to dig an underground tunnel for the capture of the fort, the besieged should dig a ditch inside the walls so deep as to make water come out of the earth. If the digging of a ditch is considered impracticable, a number of wells may be constructed along the walls. In suspicious places along the parapet, empty pots or bronze vessels may be placed in order to find out the direction in which a tunnel is being dug by the enemy. When the direction of the tunnel is discovered a counter-tunnel should be constructed; or having made a hollow passage to the tunnel, it may be filled with poisonous smoke or water.

Conclusion

The means recommended in the *Arthaśāstra* for averting danger to the state and for achieving success over hostile elements might often appear to be obnoxious from the moral point of view. It should not be forgotten, however, that the use of such means is intended against intractable enemies of the state. Its justification is that it is necessary in the interests of the state. One of the characteristic features of the *Arthaśāstra* is that questions of morality are not allowed to intrude when policies are considered that are to be pursued towards enemies of the state, those who jeopardize its security and independence. This is a position that is tacitly recognised as necessary when it is a question of practical politics. Even when certain actions may be regarded as morally unjustifiable, they are in actual practice resorted to in the supreme interests of the state. Objections that some political actions are unethical assume that politics are a function of ethics. But in practical politics such a proposition is never accepted. Every state regards what it considers its own interests as supreme and in their defence often resorts to actions that appear unethical. The dream that politics must be thoroughly ethical may perhaps be realised at some future date. It is, however, unfair in the meanwhile to condemn an author of over two thousand years ago—who was the most realistic and practical and wrote on this subject—for not recommending something that is found impracticable in politics even to-day.

CONTEMPORARY MILITARY RELEVANCE OF THE *ARTHAŚĀSTRA*

War is a constituent element of the history of mankind. Resort to violence has been widespread and very nearly universal with little relationship of its frequency and severity to the characteristics of peoples and their geographic locations. Control of armed forces rests with the state as the sovereign territorial group. The state also has effective control within its territory and is able to limit the use of the armed forces, when it controls violence. The margin of superiority is generally assumed to determine the degree to which violence can be limited. It is also generally accepted that the degree to which a margin of superiority is predominant the less likelihood of it being challenged through war. Also, if there is a challenge, the greater the margin of superiority the more quickly can the challenge, in theory, be suppressed and less sustained the violence. The rationale for having strong armed forces is thus axiomatic. Kautilya understood this and enunciated many military strategies in the *Arthaśāstra*. Also, he does not seem to have made much distinction between military strategy and statecraft. He believed that warfare is an extension and an integral part of statecraft. He has covered an array of strategies over a vast canvas from actual fighting and planning, to training and deceit. Some of these will be discussed in a contemporary context.

Military strategy is the manoeuvring of military forces to support political assertions and demands. It involves both the threat and the use of military force. The essence of strategy is the relationship between the two. This relationship is not a simple one, because of the reciprocal nature of the threat of force in battle. The problem of supporting political demands or goals through the threat or implied use of force is complicated greatly by the implied use of force to resist the demand. When this occurs, the political problem is immediately complemented by a military problem which may, or may not, become paramount, depending upon the nature of the resistance. In any case the mutual threat of force adds a military dimension, beyond the purely political aspects. It is the task of strategy to overcome the military threat, and at the same time establish the foundations for a political solution in accordance with the nature of the political demands.

Strategy is distinguished from tactics by the fact that it deals with more than the military goal. Tactics encompasses the conduct of fire and movement, the command of forces in battle; strategy goes beyond tactics, although including tactics as a part of itself. Strategy is concerned with relating military operations to political goals. In this sense it deals not alone with the techniques of combat but also with rationalising the objectives in combat with concrete steps to provide the basis for a political settlement. It is important to note that in this context strategy differs from tactics not simply in order of magnitude but also in nature. Although tactics is classified as a subordinate element of strategy, the real difference between the two is in kind as well as magnitude.

In an increasingly complex world, the missions of the armed forces are correspondingly more diverse and complex than ever before. In times of peace and tension, the armed forces are a powerful instrument of the nation's foreign policy. In times of crisis and conflict, they are the foremost expression of the nation's will and intent. Suffice to say that the expectations of a nation from its military are diverse and wide-ranging. Therefore, modern warfare is not restricted to war alone but encompasses military, political, economic and the diplomatic aspects.

Planning a Campaign

Organised warfare implies the conduct of systematic military operations. It is distinguished above all by one identifying characteristic—organisation. Modern warfare is differentiated from its earlier forms by the expansion of technology. Kautilya's most striking doctrine is his discussion of planning a campaign. He discusses the factors to be taken into account before the king/state decides that it is in the state's interest to commence the campaign. Kautilya brings out the various facets of planning a campaign and enunciates eight factors which are to be critically considered for determining whether a campaign would end in success, prior to making preparations for war. These include:

(a) Relative strengths of power, place and time;
(b) Seasons for marching on an a campaign;
(c) Employment of troops;
(d) Revolts and the rebellion in the rear;
(e) Calculation of losses, expenses;
(f) Likely dangers of treachery;
(g) Assessment of dangers; and
(h) Overcoming of dangers.

Power. According to Kautilya, the most important factor in the planning and decision-making for conducting a military campaign is power. Power includes an analysis of the military and economic strength of the adversary, as well as his intellectual power. He stressed on the ability of the army to carry out a objective analysis and not to be swayed by emotion or opinions. He even lists out the order of the three constituents of power—intellectual power, military strength, and morale—in decreasing order of importance. Kautilya advised that, though the mightier king may be endowed with better war machinery and could muster heroic fighters, the power of good analysis and judgement (which include intelligence and the knowledge of politics—the two eyes of the king) are superior to sheer military strength. Force in present day warfare encompasses tangible (personnel, weapons, mobility, fire power and logistics) and intangible elements (leadership, morale, discipline, training, doctrine and motivation). The easiest aspects of military affairs to quantify are weapons and their effects. Weapons have well-known and easily measurable physical characteristics; they obey the standard laws of physics. It is the variables of combat which bring the intangible elements into play. The human element is given the highest importance by Kautilya, unlike modern thinkers who give more importance to the military inventory. The intangible human elements are difficult to quantify and hence tend to tilt the balance if not correctly assessed. Hence to compare two opponents as emphasised in the *Arthaśāstra* , their power in all aspects needs to be compared.

Place/Terrain. The employment of the various arms and services of the army are contingent upon the terrain over which they are to be utilised. The timing of their use also needs to be given due importance with respect to terrain. Kautilya articulated that the terrain being used for conflict should be unsuitable for the enemy and suitable for own operations. This brings into focus the present trend of preparing the battlefield. The importance of terrain to manoeuvre is axiomatic. Present-day conventional warfare propagates that the free movement of one's forces and the space available are crucial for success in war. Terrain features are exploited as barriers to lomit or canalize the advance of attacking echelons and provide cover for defending troops. From a manoeuvre standpoint, distinctive terrain features appear either as avenues of approach or as obstacles. The importance of space was evident to Kautilya (except the new concept of cyberspace). However his postulate that on each kind of space the king should undertake such works to increase his power is still relevant.

Time/Campaigning Season. Kautilya has laid stress on timing and selection of season for an expedition. Climate and the time or duration of a campaign is of great importance. His concept of space is replicated as he articulates that the time of conflict should be unsuitable for the enemy and suitable for own operations. He also states the various kinds of warfare and weapons to be used in different seasons, e.g. an army consisting mostly of elephants should be used in rains or when plenty of water is available, camels and horses may be used in little rain or areas with muddy water. In manoeuvre the mobility and weight of a force are relative, not only to each other and between the opposing forces but also with respect to the different elements in each force. Operational factors in modern warfare give serious consideration to the calculation and consideration of time which gets further divided into preparation time, warning time, reaction time, decision-cycle time etc. Durations of the campaign and the interval between two consecutive operations should be kept short for maintaining a high tempo. This is brought out by Kautilya when he recommends that, 'whenever the king is superior, he shall not waste any time and should proceed against the enemy whenever by doing so the enemy can be weakened or crushed'. Due to the advent of new technologies the pace of warfare is increasing and new technologies are enlarging the area of combat. Consequently, the time factor is being compressed. The critical evaluation of time, and weather parameters and advice for planning a long, medium and short war as given in the *Arthaśāstra* remain relevant even today.

Troop Mobilisation. Kautilya lays down the criteria for mobilising different kinds of troops e.g. the standing army is to be chosen if the threat is great and from well trained troops, however the territorial army is to be chosen if the enemy is weak. The militia is to be mobilised if the enemy is weak and it is only a law and order problem. Friendly or allied forces are to be used when the king and the ally have the same objective. Jungle tribes or irregulars should be used when there is a gain to the king, whether they win or lose in fighting the enemy—'just as a *Chandala* stands to benefit when a wild dog fights a wild boar'. Combat potential is converted into combat power by mobilisation of troops and start of conflict. Kautilya preferred an army of trained *Kshatriyas* or a large force composed of *Sudras* and *Vaishyas*. He was the first Brahmin to advocate using the lower castes to fight wars. It was, perhaps the precursor to the concept of a volunteer army. It is aphoristic that the role of the leader has two fundamental facets—group solidarity and coordinated operations. The loyalty and faith which the members feel for the group are sentimentalised in the symbols of leadership. The composition of the force is an operational matter as long as the troops are disciplined and their activities integrated into the overall plan.

Rebellions. Kautilya discusses issues relating to revolts and the rebellion in the rear. This could be akin to the eruption of insurgencies. Kautilya advocates calculation of losses, expenses and gains and the likely dangers of uprisings in the rear. It suggests planning or initiating military action in the right political environment. A military organisation is an integrated structure which provides for the conduct of conflict with violence, through integration of its own activities, but which bases its authority upon the premise that it functions as an extension of the political authority of the state.

The Relationship between Power, Place and Time. Kautilya has clearly enunciated that though each of these components is important in warfare, none is more important than the other and all are interdependent. The fact that Kautilya understood the space-time-force paradigm and its dynamics is a revelation. He postulated that only when the king finds that he is superior in power space and time shall he proceed against the enemy. "Force is important for a campaign; just as the collision of an unbaked mud-vessel with a similar vessel is destructive to both, so war with an equal king brings ruin to both...place (space) is important as a dog, seated in a convenient place, can drag a crocodile and a crocodile in low ground can drag a dog...time is critical as during the daytime the crow kills the owl and at night the owl the crow." Therefore, correct forces need to be deployed in the correct terrain at a time of their choosing for maximum effect. The analogy of the crocodile being dragged by a dog would refer to a vastly superior force being inexorably drawn away from their base into an area of operations that is favourable to the smaller enemy e.g. large conventional forces being drawn into fighting in urban areas. The object of battle is victory; the conduct of fire and movement as well as creation of shock is only the means to an end. The form of influence which can be exercised is through initiative i.e. the freedom and capability (will) to act, and on the other a constringent or inducement to respond to these acts in some way, although not necessarily in any given manner.

Assessment of Dangers. If the military solution in war depends ultimately upon decisive victory, the optimum strategy is one which brings about decisive battle under favourable conditions, with a minimum of delay. To fundamental principles comprehend the whole plan of war and serve as a guide for everything else. The first is: : to trace the weight of the enemy's power back to as few centres of gravity as possible, to one if it can be done; again, to confine the attack against these centres of gravity to as few principal undertakings a possible, to one if possible; lastly, to keep all secondary undertakings as subordinate as possible. In a word, the first principle is: to act with as much concentration as possible. The second principle is: to act as swiftly as possible: therefore to permit no delay or detour without sufficient reasons.

It seems clear that such a formulation as the above does not exclude a strategy of limited aim. At the same time it does provide for applying, within the limit of total capabilities, whatever force is necessary to overthrow the enemy if he continues to resist and defies the political assertions or demands that brought about the war. From the viewpoints of the military commanders supporting the political demands, whether the war can be limited or not depends in the first instance upon the nature of the political demands; whether it will remain limited depends in the second instance upon the nature of the resistance—upon the level of forces which the enemy can introduce into the combat effectively. In the engagement of the military forces the notion of impending battle regulates the developing pattern of manoeuvre, and it is not until there is some stabilising of the military situation at the tactical level through a reduction of the mutual threat of force, that there can be any opportunity for real political negotiations, short of capitulation or collapse by one of the opponents. If there is to be a settlement short of complete overthrow or exhaustion, it can be expected to come only through political initiative so long as both military forces retain an effective operational capability. In accordance with a concept that assigns military forces the responsibility for supporting national goals, successful strategy implies the use of force in the most effective manner to accomplish that end.

Internal Security

Physical Security. The security of own kingdom consisted of physical security and also the capability to prevent treachery, revolts and rebellion. The frontier post and forts (consisting of mountains, rivers, jungle and deserts) provided physical security. The importance given to internal security was immense. Demobilisation of troops was carried out in times of peace to save money and they were mobilised again for conquests. However the forces guarding the forts, royal property and the kings own guards were never disbanded, thus ensuring the importance of internal security. Kautilya was extremely wary of revolts, rebellion and the ability of spies to influence the people by wrong news/treachery.

Control over the Army. Various means were utilised by the king to maintain control over his army including the Chiefs by paying them well, keeping them under surveillance and testing their integrity to prevent any rebellion. Some of the measures included were:

(a) They were paid well to prevent them from being tempted by bribes by the enemy.

(b) They were kept under surveillance of clandestine agents, especially to see that they did not succumb to the instigations of the enemy.

(c) Their integrity was tested to weed out the cowardly.

(d) The wings of the Army were kept under the control of

more than one chief so that mutual fear and suspicion would ensure their loyalty.

(e) Those suspected of treachery were posted to remote areas while their families were kept in the capital as hostages.

Imperativeness of Security. Kautilya believed that offensive action is based on defensive power. His insistence of for internal security clearly underlined underlines the fact that before forces are committed to the main task all own vital and vulnerable targets should be secured. In fact he even advises the king to keep the treasury and army under his control. In case of a threat of revolt, Kautilya advises the king to remain behind in the capital and allow his Commander to lead a campaign. This, coupled with the fact that he attached great importance to controlling his army, brings out the fact that internal security must be the sound foundation for a successful campaign.

Threat of Coup. Kautilya advised the king not to leave military matters entirely to others and be involved in it. He paid great importance to the training of the army and to the loyalty of the soldiers. Towards this end he advocated the use of spies especially from threat of a coup. Kautilya recommended that secret agents, prostitutes, artisans and actors as well as elders of the army should ascertain with diligence, the loyalty or disloyalty of soldiers.

Types of Warfare

Kautilya has described four types of war as follows:

(a) ***Mantrayuddha* or War by Counsel**. This is the exercise of diplomacy to win wars. It is to be utilised when the king is in a weaker position and engaging in battle would not be wise or beneficial.

(b) ***Prakasayuddha* or Open Warfare**. This is the normal form of warfare. Open warfare, Kautilya declared, is most righteous, but he was willing to use any and all kinds of warfare to achieve consolidation and expansion of the kingdom. Kautilya advised the king that "when he is superior in troops, and when he is on land suitable to himself, he should engage in an open fight. In the reverse case, he should resort to concealed fighting." This was quite unlike the teachings in the Indian epics which emphasised *dharmayudha* or ethical warfare. Thus the only rule in warfare is that there are no rules. In an interaction between two opposing forces, the reaction of each to the other is dependent in part upon judgements as to the implications of acts of the other. These judgements are formed from the information available, from an analysis of its probable significance, and from an evaluation of the probable effect of these acts taken in conjunction with possible counteractions.

(c) ***Kutayuddha* or Concealed Warfare**. This form of warfare includes psychological warfare and treachery in the enemy's camp. In contemporary parlance it can be termed guerrilla warfare. It would, to a degree, also include the use of surprise and deception. Surprise in its military sense is best understood in the context of an expanding sphere of activity. Essentially surprise implies that one or the other adversary becomes aware of an action under such circumstances that time becomes the primary constraint limiting the adequacy of response. Surprise and deception may be an important corollary to taking the initiative, but it should not be viewed as something apart or as a substitute for it.

(d) ***Gudayuddha* or Clandestine/Silent War**. This type of war is waged by covert means to achieve the objective. It includes means to win without fighting the battle by means such as assassinating the enemy. Also called silent war, it is a kind of warfare with another kingdom in which the king and his ministers—and unknowingly, the people—all act publicly as if they were at peace with the opposing kingdom, but all the while secret agents and spies are assassinating important leaders in the other kingdom, creating divisions among key ministers and classes, and spreading propaganda and disinformation. In silent warfare, secrecy is paramount and the king can prevail only by "maintaining secrecy when striking again and again." In contemporary formulation, the term could also indicate the prevailing conditions of a cold war.

Military Organisation

Military organisation is covered in great detail in the *Arthaśāstra*. Maintenance of the state's armies, troops and the organisational structure of various components are still valid. The organisation was based on the number ten and as today we follow the relationship of three. In olden times, since space was limited, it was perhaps possible to have a commander controlling ten subordinate commanders. A hierarchical methodology of command and control is axiomatic.

Managing the Army. Kautilya warns against calamities which adversely affect the functioning of the army which include not giving due honours, insufficient salaries and emoluments, low morale etc. He states that armies should never be abandoned, left leaderless or totally merged into someone else's army and it should always have adequate reinforcements. He further warns against calamities which adversely affect the functioning of the army. He makes an incisive observation when he states that an unhonoured army, an unpaid army, or an exhausted army will fight if honoured, paid and allowed to relax but a dishonoured army with resentment in its heart will not do so. According importance to leadership he avers that an army repulsed will fight if rallied by heroic men unlike an army abandoned by its chief. This is as truism that is relevant even today. A pre-requisite for an effective leader is to keep in mind two fundamental elements—the mission and the people.

The secret service (*gudapurusha*) had three principal strategic objectives. The first was that it kept the ruler informed of developments within and without the empire. The second was that the secret service conducted covert operations aimed at undermining both internal and external enemies. And third, the secret service was mandated with the maintenance of the internal discipline and loyalty of the bureaucracy and military. A major operational principle that was not to be violated except in cases of extreme emergency was that intelligence reports from three different sources were needed for the state to authorize action.

Algorithim of Victory

When two kings are at war, he advises his king to sue for peace with a stronger king, accept the peace offer of an equally strong king and to destroy the weaker king. He justifies going to war by the natural enemy concept which states that if the conqueror does not eliminate the enemy, the enemy will eliminate him. After victory it is vitally important to consolidate on newly-acquired territory so as to be able to embark on further conquests. He clarifies that a defeated army should never be harassed to the point of making it so desperate that it will return to fight with vengeance.

Oligarchies/Coalitions

A whole section is dedicated to oligarchies or confederacy. In the present world such a communion is exhibited by coalition forces. While accepting that these coalitions are strong entities Kautilya frames various means to fight and put up resistance against them. As an oligarchy is defined as an unassailable cohesive unit, sowing dissension, using deceit, treachery and playing on the differences amongst them has been suggested as measures to defeat them.

Strategies for a Weak King

Kautilya has written extensively on the response of a weak king when being attacked by a stronger king. When confronted by a superior power Kautilya advices the weak king to find a way to survive to fight another day, preserving "his body, not wealth; for, what regret can there be for wealth that is impermanent?" Kautilya did not however expect the weak king to give in to the conqueror without a fight and recommended various measures which included use of 'diplomatic or concealed warfare' and instigating a revolt in the enemy camp. As a desperate measure he even advocated a powerful speech offering a mixture of moral exhortation and arguments to be given to the superior king.

People and Popular Support

Kautilya maintained that people were more important than forts and armies. As he put it, "one should only seek a fortress with men." He urged the king to be popular with the people and to endeavour to secure the welfare of his subjects. The *Arthaśāstra* has emphasised on not causing harm even to the subjects of the enemy king. In fact extraordinary measures are recommended to win over a defeated population. Their customs had to be respected and their gods had to be revered by the new king. Looting and carrying away spoils of war was forbidden.

Dealing with Insurgencies

Kautilya's Thumb Rule. An analysis of most insurgencies in the world shows that Kautilya was accurate in his belief that the greatest cause of insurgencies was societal discontent and advocates that the state attach great importance to the well being of the people -"if they become impoverished, they become greedy and rebellious". He also averred that "an internal rebellion is more dangerous than an external threat because it is like nurturing a viper in one's bosom".

The types of rebellions (insurgencies) were classified in their seriousness based on the affected region and who were their sponsors. The similarities in the methods used today and those espoused by Kautilya are striking. Kautilya proposed the use of four instruments of state power—Conciliation (Diplomatic), Dissension (Informational), Force (Military) and Gifts (Economic), which are the instruments used by states even today (DIME). Although application of his principles would depend on the extenuating circumstances of a case, his thumb-rule gives us a basic framework for planning a counter insurgency operation.

A well-governed state will have less to fear from subversion and revolt and be in a better position to disrupt the domestic stability of its adversaries. It would also be able to move with greater surety toward the execution of any foreign or defence policy related tasks that necessitate the large-scale mobilisation of economic and military power. Faster, enthusiastic, properly-trained and well-remunerated bureaucracies reduce the friction inherent in converting the intentions of the rulers into effects on the ground. A state that neglects the quality of the administrative elite and institutions upon which the execution of policy depends does so at the greatest possible peril to itself.

A comparable peril against which a state must guard is the tendency to allow the individual components of state power to fragment the making and execution of policy. For Kautilya, whose emphasis is on the integrated nature of state power, it would be the height of absurdity for the administrative, economic, military and intelligence assets of a state to be deployed without a proper coherent vision and understanding of the common goals they seek to achieve. For, the individual components of state power to be thus divided and operate at cross-purposes would breed chaos and indiscipline within the state. The synthesising element is that of leadership—political, bureaucratic, military, and intelligence. Without effective leadership, disorder will prevail within the state apparatus and gravely diminish the ability of the state to either control or effectively respond to challenges. Unless a country has an exceptionally high margin of geographic security, the consequences of such discord are likely to be fatal.

In situations of urban warfare (against a fortified enemy city), Kautilya explicitly stated that indiscriminate bombing (use of fire) would be counterproductive: "...fire shall not be used at all. For fire is a divine calamity whose effects are unpredictable; it is a destroyer of uncountable numbers of people and wealth. Even when captured, such a fort would only give rise to further losses." The applicability to modern day urban counter-insurgency is implicit; the application of mechanised warfare and firepower (or excessive airpower) would almost never work in an urban environment as a military victory would still leave the combat zone broken and the population distraught.

Conclusion

Kautilya regarded the period before the actual fighting began as critical to the outcome. It was vital that the ruler and his advisors be able and willing to undertake a dispassionate and rational appreciation of the total assets of their state in relation to the enemy (or enemies) modified by the contributions of allies. Thus, geography, timing, seasonal variations, mobilisation schedules, preparing for internal rebellions and discontent, estimating the material losses in relation to strategic gains, and the risks involved to the stability of the dynasty all had to be carefully weighed. There was no point in attacking a more powerful state without first consulting one's allies. Similarly, committing troops to a limited engagement without factoring the possibility of escalation and the likely losses was to be avoided. While the military was trained and drilled into believing in itself and the power of positive thinking, for the ruler and his senior servants, optimism was a dangerous and potentially catastrophic luxury. Indeed, for Kautilya the power of solid advice was greater than military strength, and by combining superior intelligence and comprehension of politics the conqueror could prevail against militarily more powerful adversaries.

We have thus in the text of the *Arthaśāstra* as full an advice on how to foil an ambitious king's imperialistic designs as on how to conquer and build an empire. While it sets forth the ideal of conquest, it takes into account all possible situations in which any state may find itself and offers advice on what courses are open to it and which course it would be preferable to follow in any given situation. Its teaching is intended for all kings, for the weak king being attacked, the *yatavya*, the *hina*, the *abaliyas*, the *dandopanata*, as much as for the strong, ambitious king, the *jyayas*, the *balavat*, the *dandopanayin*. That is what makes it so comprehensive.

It is because of Kautilya's endeavour to imagine and provide for all possible situations which a state may have to face in its relations with foreign states that we sometimes find details that might appear to be of little significance. To regard this as an indication of his pedantry is, however, to misunderstand the nature and scope of this work. It is not a treatise on general principles, but a work concerned with recommending practicable policies in any conceivable situation that may arise in actual political life. And its visualisation of such situations and the courses that are then open to a state is characterised by a realism that is altogether unique. And its teaching has not lost its relevance in these matters even to-day.

In today's world, the challenges of global security are no different from the challenges that vexed the Mauryan Empire in 300 BC. A cogent and dispassionate analysis of the *Arthaśāstra* reveals stark similarities between the problems faced by Kautilya's ideal state and the modern scourge of terrorism and insurgencies. Scientific techniques tempered by the application of high technology have failed to dent the practitioners of these reprehensible deeds; it is perhaps time for humanity to turn the clock of learning backward and delve into its past to obtain an ancient remedy for this modern malaise. Present day warfare adheres to ancient patterns. The truism that 'those who forget the lessons of history are condemned to repeat it', is most true in the world of military affairs.

The *Arthaśāstra* is testimony to the constant and unchanging nature of war. Studies of military history show that certain features of conflict and warfare constantly recur; that relationships between type of action and success often remain the same; that certain circumstances and moments have time and time again, proved decisive. The past being a prologue underscores the relevance and significance of studies of military history such as propagated by the *Arthaśāstra*.

REFLECTIONS

The only exception to India's absence of central canonical texts on strategy and warfare has been the ancient classic, Kautilya's *Arthaśāstra.* It is, however, not a theoretical treatise on political science. It does not directly concern itself with the question of the origin of the state, its nature or its functions. It does not inquire how some people come to rule over others and how or why the majority of people are content to be governed by a few. Nor does it refer to the various forms that a state organisation is found to take or discuss their relative advantages and disadvantages. What it says on such questions is only incidental. Its primary concern is with matters of practical administration. However, it is possible to trace some sort of a theoretical basis for the teaching of the *sastra*. Monarchy is assumed to be the normal form of government. The entire teaching of the *sastra* is addressed to the king, the single ruler of a state. The original state of nature is imagined to be one of total anarchy, where might alone was right. People agreed to pay taxes and to be ruled by one person in order that they may be able to enjoy security and well-being (*yoga-kshema*). However, it is no theory of a social contract. Be that as it may, it is important to inquire as to how and why the ideals and content embodied in the *Arthaśāstra* slipped out of Indian consciousness over the millennia?

Kautilya's *Arthaśāstra* (variously translated as "science of politics" or "treatise on polity") is acknowledged by Indian scholars as the most important ancient Indian text on strategy. Kautilya is still an inspiration to modern Indian strategic and military thought. The *Arthaśāstra* is a complex and subtle work, and as such is vulnerable to selective reading and interpretation. This leads some to focus on the worst in the text and to overlook the subtle and not-so-subtle warnings about the dangers of war and the need for prosperity, good governance, and legitimate rule to maintain power. Also, the *Arthaśāstra* does not form the whole of Indian strategic tradition. Whereas the *Arthaśāstra* emphasizes both political flexibility and military mobility, an older tradition represented by another Indian classic text, the Mahabharata, emphasizes annihilation of the enemy through systematic attrition.

Power, according to the *Arthaśāstra*, is the object of interstate relations, and dissension and force are the natural state of international relations. Power is relative and must be maximised both in absolute and relative terms, for survival and success. There is a clear *realpolitik* in Kautilya, as well as an offensive doctrine. The *Arthaśāstra* propounded teachings on the pursuit of power through *realpolitik*, the recommended use of offensive force, deception, treachery, assassination, and deceit, and the view that conquest and the establishment of hegemony is the proper policy of the "good" leader.

Perhaps the most commonly cited idea from Kautilya is the concept of *mandalas*, or circles. Those closer in the circle, on the borders of the state, will be enemies. Those farther away will be allies. This discussion of natural enemies and natural allies has led some to interpret Kautilya's work as consistent with balance-of-power politics. Kautilya's idea of concentric circles is not meant to be one of fixed geographic relationships. Rather, for Kautilya, *mandalas* apply to relationships of power, influence, and interest, not only geographic proximity. Relationships are not so fixed that all border states must be enemies, although Kautilya believed that bordering states were more likely to be enemies or objects of conquest than not. Kautilya explicitly advocates conquest and holds the opinion that the best leader is a conqueror who actively seeks to maximize power at all times, and who also constantly prepares for war either actively or passively.

Kautilya counsels on matters broader than war alone. He also notes that war is dangerous and uncertain, and that if there is no prospect of one's decline relative to an enemy, then peace (while continuing to maximize prosperity and the fruits of conquest) is preferable to war, Furthermore, generating and sustaining wealth and political legitimacy are also critical. Kautilya was deeply concerned with the moral quality of leaders, the welfare of the people, justice, and the legitimacy of the regime. In his view, justice and legitimacy in foreign policy, as well as military prowess, were necessary for a leader's success.

Historical Backdrop

The history of ancient India is one of almost continuous warfare, broken by occasional periods of short-lived peace. The doctrine of *mandala*, which epitomises the Hindu conception of inter-state relations, is essentially a doctrine of strife and struggle. It was no mere abstract theory, but embodied the experience of political leaders through countless generations. The factors which contributed to the frequency of warfare included usurpation of the kingdom, abduction of women, seizure of provinces and portions of territory, carrying away of goods and treasures, arrogance, morbid sense of honour, molestation, extinction of learning, destruction of property, violation of laws, prostration of the regal powers, influence of evil destiny, necessity of helping friends and allies, disrespectful demeanour, elimination of friends, want of compassion, disaffection of the *mandala*, and common eagerness for possession of the same object.

A more potent factor was the Hindu ideal of *vijigisu*. Ancient texts inculcate times without number that fighting constituted the essential function of a king, and that pacificism and kingship were a contradiction in terms. A king's highest duty was not to shun war, but to get ready to smite his foes. Like a snake swallowing up mice," says Usanas, a pre-Kautilyan author on politics, "the earth swallows the king who refuses to fight and the *Brahmin* who is unduly attached to wives and children." "Like a fisherman," says Bharadwaja, "who cannot become prosperous except by catching and killing fish; a king can never attain prosperity without tearing the vitals of his enemy and performing other violent deeds. The armed might of your foe should be completely destroyed by ploughing it up and mowing it down or otherwise afflicting it by famine, starvation and thirst." Elsewhere it is emphasised that "no respect is due to a king who does not somehow or other subdue his enemies. He sinks like a cow in the mud, and is as helpless as an ant. "There is," it is said time and again, "absolutely no rule but conflict for one of the warrior caste."

This incessant harping on war as an instrument of policy was not without purpose. In the congeries of small states into which India was habitually divided, often without natural frontiers marking them off into separate geographical units, military strength was the only guarantee for the continued existence of a kingdom. It was a guarantee not merely against strong rivals in the neighbourhood, but against the subtler forces of internal disintegration. But there was perhaps a deeper reason behind this ceaseless advocacy of war. The Hindus, it is well known, had evolved a synthesis out of the heterogeneous mass of customs, traditions, values, tastes and beliefs, held by the various communities and races inhabiting this vast sub-continent. This synthesis was already a well-established fact before the rise of Maurya Empire, and was never seriously disturbed till the advent of Islam. But there was nothing corresponding to this cultural unity in the political sphere. From very early times, therefore, men longed to set up a common political organisation for the whole country. This longing gave birth to the concept of *chakravartin* or *sarvabhauma* (paramount sovereign). Kautilya felt that monarchy, at its highest, should have an empire extending right up to natural boundaries; it should be territorially all-embracing, up to the very ends uninterrupted, and constitute and establish one state and administration in the land up to the seas. Kautilya defined a *chakravartin* as one holding sway over the whole land extending north to south from the Himalayas to the sea and measuring a thousand *yojanas* across.

Whether they consciously believed it or not, most of the great warlords of ancient India seem to have acted in pursuance of this idea. The motive force behind the endless campaigns and expeditions of the Mauryas, the Guptas and succeeding rulers, does not seem to have been mere ambition, a passion for conquering for the sake of conquering, but a conscious or unconscious urge to bring the whole country under a single hegemony. The success attained was often partial and temporary because the forces of disintegration were too strong to be permanently surmounted. The vastness of the country, the difficulty of intercommunication, the selfish ambition of local chiefs, the lack of general ideas and common interests, the almost total absence of all the sources from which a government must draw its life and strength, rendered all attempts at empire-building in fructuous. But nonetheless the ideal was there, consciously held by some, unconsciously by almost all; and its existence accounts for, to some extent at any rate, the frequency of internecine strife in India.

Concurrently with the king's duty to fight, ancient writers have stressed and eulogised the soldier's duties as second to none. The *Shantiparva* says: "Among men the highest duties are those performed by the warrior caste. The whole world is subject to the might of their arms. All the duties, principal and subordinate, of the three other orders are dependent for their observance upon the duties of the warrior." And the essence of the warrior's duty, like that of the king, lies in fighting. No matter how challenged, the warrior, who is true to his salt, must respond. He must, moreover, never think of fleeing from the battlefield. The gods headed by *Indra* send calamities unto those who forsake their comrades in battle, and come home with unwounded limbs. Not only do they get disrepute in this world, but are condemned to eternal hell after death." The man who died a soldier's death on the battle-field was promised forgiveness of all his sins.

The teachings of the ancient authors asserted that the great position that is acquired by sages after long and tedious penances is also attained by warriors who meet death in war. This was at once penance, virtue, and eternal religion. The man, who does not flee from battle, does at once perform the duties of the four *ashramas*. It was believed that only two men go beyond the solar sphere in heaven, viz. the austere ascetic and the soldier who is killed in battle with his face to the foe. Such was and is the burden of the warrior; he must kill or be killed in the fight; there is to be no third alternative. If he conquers the foe, he attains fame and glory in earthly life; if he is defeated and killed in the fray, he is transported straightaway to heaven.

There are reasons to think that these maxims, which appealed at once to the basest and the highest in man, left a deep impress on the life of the military communities. They prepared the warriors for suffering and pain, restraint and violence, blood and tears, and to embrace the horrors of destruction and terrors of death cheerfully.

The code of military honour included other articles besides victory or death on the battle-field. Wounded and unarmed opponents, for instance, were to be considered as exempt from slaughter. It was also regarded as a gross offence to refuse quarter to an armed enemy who had ceased fighting and asked for mercy. Such a person might be imprisoned, but never wounded or slain. Similarly it was forbidden to slay one who was weary or asleep, one who was walking along a road unaware of danger, one who was greatly enfeebled by wounds or stricken with grief, one who lingered trustfully, as well as the insane, the wounded, servants, camp-followers, old men, children and women. Moreover, prisoners of war were to be cared for and. treated with humanity. Captured opponents were to be either sent to their homes, or if brought to the victor's quarters, should have their wounds attended to by skilful surgeons, and when cured, set at liberty. Further, weapons which caused unnecessary pain or which inflicted more suffering than was indispensable to overcome the foe were condemned. When fighting with his foes the warrior was not to strike with instruments concealed, with barbed or poisoned weapons, or the points of which are blazing with fire. The seizure or destruction of enemy property unless imperatively demanded by the necessities of war was also prohibited, Temples and their property in places under military occupation and the private property of individual citizens were on no account to be seized.

While it is a truism that rules are often forgotten in the bitterness of conflict, and Emperor Ashoka's campaign against Kalinga is a glaring example, Kautilya did advocate the use of fraud and treachery in warfare. The fact that ends justify the means was elaborated upon by Lord Krishna also. On the whole, however, it would seem that wars in ancient India were characterised by less violence and savagery than wars elsewhere. There is no recorded instance of wanton and cold-blooded atrocity. Such incidents of war as the indiscriminate slaughter of all men of military age or the enslavement of women and children of the conquered state were hardly known. These wars, moreover, did not usually lead to any great political changes. On the whole, the chiefs were considerate of each other's rights. It was a well-established maxim of statecraft that a victor should acquiesce in the continuance of the laws, beliefs and customs of the vanquished peoples, and that instead of seeking the extermination of the defeated dynasties; he should be content with their submission and tribute. This policy was one of 'uprooting and replanting', according to the Kautilyan ideal of *dharmavijaya*, and the typical Hindu method of creating unity out of diversity in the political sphere.

The history of India offers numerous illustrations of the application of this policy. Conscious that this was perhaps the best way of harmonising the conflicting interests of imperialism and local independence, empire-builders seem to have transformed this policy into a tradition. Thus a ruler would go to war for conquest, but when a king subdued a neighbouring state, he placed over it a man belonging to the family of the fallen prince, who carried on the government in the name of the conqueror. The inhabitants would not suffer it to be otherwise. The pursuit of this policy, however, led to the growth of a class of feudatory chiefs. It is also the reason why some of the princely families in India boast of a long and illustrious ancestry.

Broadly speaking, the wars seldom involved any grave disturbance either to the social equilibrium or the economic life of the people. It is important to remember that in India the social, economic and religious life of the people pursued its course irrespective of the activities of the state, and, consequently, wars and campaigns were generally regarded as the business of chiefs and kings and the professionals who chose to serve them. The bulk of the people was indifferent to the fortunes of war, and did not believe that they had any great interest whether their king was 'X' or 'Y'. This was partly due to the growth of despotism, which became the prevailing form of government, and the consequent dissociation of the people from the activities of the state, and partly to the comparative immunity from violence and molestation which the wealth-producing classes in the country enjoyed. This peculiar trait of Indian warfare has been seen over the centuries that when a battle was going on, the neighbouring cultivators might be observed quietly pursuing their work. It was, perhaps out of the notion that the common labourer could be of help to both armies. The concept of a 'nation-at-arms' or the idea of nationhood was not known. Might was generally right and he could rule received allegiance. He whose rule failed found that allegiance transferred to someone else. There was nothing immoral, improper or untoward about this.

A question which inevitably faces every student of India's past, especially of her military system, is—what were the causes which led to the fall of the Hindus? Why did the Indian states fall easy prey to the Muhammadan Turks in the 11th and 12th century A.D.? It is difficult to answer this question in a few paragraphs. The causes were so numerous and so involved; and were at work for so long; that the full understanding of their operation requires an extensive knowledge of the laws which govern the growth and decline of peoples. A separate book may be required for a clear expose of this subject. A brief account of the matter is made still further difficult from the fact that "the fall of the Hindu" has been very often made the subject of partial and incomplete treatment in order to prove some particular point, perhaps to make vivid the disabling effects of the doctrines of *ahimsa* and *karma* as well as to manifest the malignant influence of caste on the life of the people.

Undoubtedly, the doctrine of *ahimsa* tended to create in certain sections of the people a deep abhorrence to all forms of violence; and the theory of *karma*, as popularly interpreted, produced a fatalistic outlook and disinclination for effort. But it would be as erroneous to attribute the downfall of the Hindus to the effects of these doctrines, as it would be to ascribe to Christianity the downfall of the Roman Empire. In both cases other and deeper causes were at work, sapping the foundations of their vitality and strength; and just as the Roman empire would have fallen, as it did, even if Christianity had not found many adherents within its borders, so would the Hindu states have succumbed to the Muhammadan Turks even if they had never known the doctrines of *ahimsa* and *karma*.

Undoubtedly, the caste system exercised a pernicious influence on the life of the people. It divided the community into classes separated by intractable barriers; inhibited freedom of choice; promoted rigid divisive attributes; and impeded the growth of a common national consciousness. Nevertheless to explain the downfall of the Hindu states by this one premise is to simplify a problem which is inherently complex. It should be borne in mind that in spite of the prevalence of the caste system, Chandragupta Maurya drove out the remnants of the Greek forces under Seleucos Nikator, left behind by Alexander. Skandagupta and Yashodharman repelled the Huns, and the Hindu kingdom of Vijayanagar checked the onrush of the armies of Islam for well over two hundred years (1336 to 1556 A.D.), and the Marathas became a mighty power on the ruins of the Mughal Empire.

Some writers would have us think that the caste system, by restricting the field of recruitment, diminished the fighting strength of the Hindu states, and thus prevented them from becoming what may be called a 'nation-in-arms'. It has been already shown that the hypothesis of troops being recruited from the *Kshatriyas varna* alone has no foundation in fact; and a 'nation-in-arms' is an entirely modern concept. Nor is there much truth in the statement that caste prevented the growth of a feeling that fighting for or defending one's own country was everyone's business and not of a particular class of people. Such consciousness was equally absent in other medieval countries and communities where the hereditary caste system of the Indian type was never known. In medieval Europe, for instance, fighting was almost wholly done by the feudal knights, and at the beginning of the modern age, by professional standing armies maintained by absolute monarchs. As in India, so in Europe down to the eighteenth century, the mass of the people seldom mixed themselves up in wars undertaken by their rulers.

The immediate causes of the fall of the Hindu states may be roughly divided into two—first, political causes; second, military. Among political causes is the fact that the commencing years of the 11th century, when the Turkish invasions beat upon the western flank of the Hindu world, were an age of decaying dynasties and of kingdoms that were failing to pieces. Northern India had split up into many small kingdoms; some of them were formed by tribal chiefs, some by military adventurers; their boundaries were shifting, and they were continually at feud with one another. This division and disunion did not make it easy for the Hindu princes to unite for a common defence to repulse the enemy. If Alexander had found India united in arms to withstand his aggression, the star of his good fortune would have culminated with the passage of the Indus. This is also applicable to Muhammad bin Kasim, Sultan Mahmud or Muhammad of Ghor. This division and disunion enabled the invaders from the north to exploit the differences within the country, for the dread of the foreigner was less than the dread of a strong neighbour.

The disruptive forces did not merely split up the country into numerous small kingdoms; they worked deeper than that. Ever since the days of the Guptas, feudal tendencies had been steadily developing in northern India, and there are good reasons to think that with the passing away of the old powerful dynasties, they reached their maturity about the 11th century A.D. The consequence was that the numerous kingdoms, into which northern India was divided, were themselves subdivided into a multitude of territorial fragments, ruled by petty chiefs or warlords.

The exact relationship between the overlord and the feudatory chiefs cannot be determined with any amount of exactitude, but in broad outline it does not seem to have been very different from what obtained between kings and their vassals in feudal Europe, i.e. while enjoying virtual autonomy in their own domains, the feudatory chiefs were bound by some kind of allegiance to their overlord and were expected to help him in times of war. There is, however, ample testimony that the feudatories were often intensely jealous of one another and did not look upon their subordination with equanimity. Whenever due to external or internal reasons there was a decline in the fortunes of the overlord's family, the more powerful among the feudatory chiefs threw off their dependence and forced the smaller vassals in their neighbourhood to change their allegiance. In fact, most of the Hindu states of this period seem to have been organised on such unstable, semi-feudal basis. Consequently the armies, with which they fought, being mostly composed of the retainers of their subordinate chiefs, lacked the uniformity of organisation and unity of control and command which is one of the essential requisites of success in war.

In consideration of the military causes, the Hindu defenders of their country, although fully equal to their assailants in courage and contempt of death, were distinctly inferior in the art of war, and for that reason lost their independence. Success in war, it is well known, depends primarily on three factors, viz. moral qualities, organisation and equipment, and leadership. An exact comparison and assessment of the Hindus and their northern antagonists on these three counts would be a difficult task. The contemporary or semi-contemporary Muhammadan chronicles, from which the story of the military operations of the time is mostly derived, are often one-sided and misleading in their statements. Yet certain facts seem to stand out in glaring light, and certain inferences are possible on the basis of those facts.

By moral qualities are meant virtues like courage, energy and determination. Although the Hindus were not lacking in these, the Muhammadan Turks seem to have possessed them in a larger measure. It is an amply-proved fact of history that during the simpler and more primitive stages of racial and tribal existence the moral qualities of courage and self-sacrifice, the complete subordination of individual advantage and individual comfort to the good of the community, are most apparent as a natural growth, and need no artificial cultivation. A civilised and prosperous community, on the other hand, is not a congenial soil for the natural development of these virtues; and the Hindus were infinitely more civilised and prosperous than the Turks. Moreover, with this rude vigour of semi-civilised barbarians they combined the fierce, religious, zeal of neo-converts. The great missionary creed of Muhammad, which to the Arabs and Persians had become a familiar matter of routine, was a source of fiery inspiration to the fresh untutored men of the steppes. To spread the faith by conquest doubled their natural zest for battle and endowed them with the devoted valour of martyrs.

The best soldier is the one who knows what he is fighting for and loves what he knows. The Turks derived strength and fortitude from the belief that they were fighting on behalf of God, whose benign protection was always with them. The Hindus, on the other hand, lacked a common ideal for which to fight and die. Nationalism and patriotism as controlling forces of history were not yet born and the very nature of their religion, which was a blend of many different elements—a synthesis of diverse customs, thoughts and beliefs—made them incapable of being fanatically intolerant. It is true that common antipathy against the foreigners, who plundered and destroyed their temples and sanctuaries, and who trampled underfoot all that they had for ages held dear and sacred, united on a few occasions some of the ruling princes in a common endeavour to oust the intruders; but it was not a strong enough cohesive force to survive a disaster or keep in check the disruptive tendencies within the country. In short, the absence of a higher, ennobling ideal rendered the Hindus incapable of combined effort, involving any continuous strain of risk or hardship.

For more than a millennium the art of war in India followed a stereotyped course, marked by no remarkable improvements in any of its branches. But the causes of this static character of the Hindu military system seem to have been deeper than a mere sense of its inherent viciousness. A similar lack of progress is noticeable in the political thought of India after Kautilya. These seem to point to the fact that the creative power of antiquity in certain spheres of speculation and achievement was exhausted. It became manifest in other spheres as centuries rolled by. Having brought civilisation up to a certain point, the Hindus seem to have been able to carry it no further. Even in those fields where the most remarkable results had been attained, as, for example, in that of philosophy and metaphysics, nothing further seemed to be possible, except to work over the old results into new forms. By the 11th century the Hindus had completely lost their genius for assimilation and absorption, and had become a grossly superstitious and vegetating people. This dismal attitude of mind, which refused either to learn or unlearn anything was at once a cause and symptom of decay. The result was stagnation; stagnation brought decay, and decay disaster. It is ever so true that a thing cannot be crushed by a blow from without until ready to perish from decay within. Can, therefore, the *Arthaśāstra* be a basis of viewing Indian strategic culture?

History has also been an important factor in shaping the Indian strategic culture. Historically, India foresees a possible revival of its ancient past as it aims to become a great power. Although independent only for 60 years, having been ruled by Mughals and British for the last many centuries, India's historical roots still originate from the Mauryan Empire of the third and fourth centuries BC. It was the golden age for Hinduism and nationalists consider it the era of Indian unity, strength and glory that stands for them as the symbol of unification of India. India was also unified again by the Mughals who also brought new military culture and new political ideas, but they did not destroy the Indian civilisation. Islam in a sense became the subcontinent's second culture, though it did not entirely escape Indian influence.

In a land as culturally, religiously, ethnically and linguistically diverse as India, the British imperialists championed the technique of 'divide and conquer' for nearly a century. To efficiently subdue India's religiously diverse provincial rulers, British political advisers split the Muslim and Hindu monarchs using deceitful practices and sowing discord amongst them. By understanding the effectiveness of such divisive political tactics in order to rule over Indian diversity, the British Raj stayed put in the vast subcontinent for close to two hundred years.

The British were the first to think explicitly about the strategic defence of South Asia as a whole. At first they developed an offensive defensive strategy by attacking India's neighbours, Burma and Afghanistan, to create buffers between British India, Russia and China. During the 200 years of the Raj, the British decided South Asia's defence policy and strategy. After independence, India adopted the policy of non-alignment and peaceful co-existence. Nehru tried to adopt a policy of establishing international influence without being a strong military power. India's non-alignment was developed on the principles of non-involvement in either of the two alliance systems and an active and independent participation in world affairs. Moreover, Nehru saw non-alignment between the superpowers during the Cold war as a vital precondition for protecting India's national interests. It became the dominant ethos of India's foreign policy.

Nehru based Indian foreign policy on "Five Principles" (*Panchsheel*), i.e. mutual respect for other nations'; territorial integrity and sovereignty; non-aggression; non-interference in internal affairs of others; equality and mutual benefit; and peaceful co-existence. These could be paraphrased as '*moralpolitik*'. These principles were, ironically, articulated in a treaty with China over Tibet in 1954, when Nehru still hoped for Sino-Indian brotherhood and leadership of a Third World of nonviolent nations, recently independent of colonial rule, eager to save the world from the Cold War superpower confrontation and possible nuclear annihilation. China and India, however, had not demarcated their borders or resolved dispute over them. The non-resolution of the competing claims over Kashmir has contributed to four wars with Pakistan. Actions in Junagadh, Hyderabad, Goa, and later in Sri Lanka and Maldives, as well as the creation of Bangla Desh show that India is sufficiently mindful of power and the utility of force.

Geography has profoundly affected India's history and culture, and therefore its strategic culture. India's strategic location, size and large population have contributed to its belief in its greatness, its pre-eminence in the Indian Ocean region and its global importance. The Himalayas and the Hindukush mountains in the north and north-east, the Bay of Bengal in the east, the Arabian Sea in the west and Indian Ocean in the south have created a giant natural entity—the Indian subcontinent. These geographic barriers have played an important role in keeping Indians within the subcontinent and allowing India to develop its own unique culture. However, the invasions from the north-west, the British rule which came from the south-east, and the partition of the sub-continent in 1947 deeply affected the subcontinents natural advantage of its geography. The partition also limited India's natural influence on Iran, Afghanistan, and Central Asia as the newly independent state of Pakistan exists squarely between India and these former neighbours.

India's Strategic Culture

Strategic culture is a relatively new concept. It is derived from the two terms 'strategy' and 'culture' and is, therefore, an amalgamation of both terms which are distinct in their own right. Several strategic thinkers have reasoned that each state has its own way to interpret, analyse and react to international events. Thus every state's threat perception and ability to respond to that threat would be different as each strategic culture has its own values, ideas, and patterns of thinking which influence its strategic behaviour and makes it distinct. Therefore, strategic culture plays a very important role in determining a state's responses to emerging threats and policy options. It helps us in understanding the strategic thinking of a nation and the logics of its security policy.

Definitions of strategic culture are the product of variations in macro-environmental factors such as historical experience, geography, societal structures and military institutions. Through it have developed concepts such as 'national character' to explain peculiar differences in state behaviour. Strategic culture entails fundamental understanding about the nature of the strategic environment, the role of force in that environment, perceptions of threat and the framing of responses to perceived threats.

History and experience are very important considerations in the rise and evolution of states, and their strategic culture. Each state has a unique, distinctive history; it draws lessons from its assessment of it and develops its statecraft in accordance with that perception. Thus, the concept of strategic culture is at the intersection of history, geography, values, beliefs and politics, and comes to explain the state behaviour in the international arena.

Strategic culture could be in various fields; however, the one that is of concern is how a state views employment or use of force or the armed forces, in various situations to achieve national interests or state goals. It guides the use of armed forces as a policy instrument. In this context, any discussion of Indian strategic culture must start by understanding the role of history.

The fact that India has been constantly subjected to foreign invasions and subjugation is ever present in the Indian mind, and this fact carries with it an intrinsic feeling of insecurity. This insecurity is premised, in part, on the belief that outside powers had been able to intervene in India because of Indian divisiveness, and their ability to play off the Indian powers against one another had been particularly successful. It is also a fact that their conquest was made easier, or possible, because of superior technology possessed by the foreigners.

When India gained freedom in 1947, it inherited the legacy of the British Raj and the influence of its strategic decision-making, its apparatus and ethos. It is the biggest state in the region and occupies a dominant position in South Asia. The future of South Asia is largely influenced by India, as being the largest country in the region. Economic and military power collectively give India a boost to its strategic and political power. As far as its economic power is concerned, since 1990 the sustained GDP growth rate hovering between 6.5 to 8 per cent is the symbol of India's rapidly growing economy. The size of the economy more than doubled during the period from 1991 to 2000, to over $500 billion, making India the tenth largest economy in the world. This progress is not only applied to the economic sphere but also to the military.

India has made tremendous strides in the past few decades and today it is a military power that has to be taken seriously. The Indian Army is a million-strong force equipped with modern technological weaponry. India possesses not only nuclear weapons but also effective delivery systems in the shape of various ballistic missiles. India's choices and actions will obviously affect the life of over one billion Indians and perhaps another two billion people around its periphery from Afghanistan and Pakistan in the west, to Nepal and China in the north, to Bangladesh and Burma (Myanmar) in the east. India's strategic behaviour will largely influence their future. Therefore, it is important to understand India's strategic thinking and it is imperative to have a clear understanding of Indian strategic culture.

Indian strategic culture could best be understood with respect to its attitudes to use of force, derived from its perception of its national historical experience, self-characterisation and from all of the many distinctively Indian experiences (of geography, political philosophy, civic culture and way of life) that characterize

India. In this context, Kautilya's teachings are a relevant factor. In consonance with Kautilyan precepts, the Indian political elite perceive India as a past and future great power that is destined to play a role not only in the subcontinent but ultimately in the Indian Ocean and on the world stage. Since independence its leadership's primary objective has been to enhance and expand India's political power. Today India considers itself as the biggest secular, democratic state of the world. The Indian leadership has played a very important role in shaping its self-image.

After attaining independence, the first Prime Minister, Jawaharlal Nehru articulated grand ambitions for a pre-eminent position in the world and his dream was to transform India into a greater India. Even when he promoted the idea of non-aligned, its purpose was to project India as an independent and sovereign state that had the right to play an independent role in global affairs. For Indian strategic thinkers the enemy is any entity whose aims or actions would deprive India of its territory or subvert its society by undermining its civilised values. Some have called this a policy of *moralpolitik* i.e. the aggressive use of morality to advance national interests. It was m*oralpolitik*, a mixture of calculation, caution and moralising which informed India's statecraft, especially in the initial decades, and helped in the accretion of means necessary for India to realise its objective of becoming an influential power.

Indian foreign policy is becoming increasingly more pragmatic, driven by strategic considerations based on realism, while an idealist inflection (the conflation of ideal and interest) still exists. In sum, while India's strategic culture does not prefer force, it is operationally not averse to use of force. The record of resort to force or threat of force speaks for itself. The very first instance was within a few months of Independence in integrating the princely states of Junagadh and Jammu and Kashmir, soon followed by police action against Hyderabad in September 1948. India evicted the Portuguese from the Goa in 1961. A 'forward policy' was followed in respect of tackling the Chinese threat across the Himalayas since 1959. It culminated in Nehru ordering the eviction of the Chinese in 1962. India expanded the scope of the 1965 conflict to the plains in Punjab from action initially restricted to Kashmir. It intervened in the internal conflict in East Pakistan in 1971 and executed a meticulously planned and prepared military operation in November-December that year. It similarly carried out the occupation of Saltoro heights in Siachen in 1984 and has maintained its occupation since. In internal security, it deployed the Army in the North East in the fifties and sixties and later in Punjab in the eighties. Its peace keeping operation in Ṣri Lanka turned into an enforcement action in 1987. It has used military exercises for signalling its resolve in the eighties to both Pakistan and China in the form of the Exercise Brasstacks and Exercise Chequerboard. The former turned into the crisis of 1987. Through the nineties the Army was deployed in J&K under laws permissive of the use of force, the Armed Forces Special Powers Act. The military evicted Pakistani intruders from Kargil in 1999. India has evolved into a nuclear power with second strike capability. It numbers among the foremost arms importers. However, almost all of India's security policy, whether nuclear or conventional, is driven by a deeply defensive idea, formulated in the context of defending territory. It has been, generally, diffident about using force as an instrument for foreign policy objectives

Indians are proud of their culture and ancient civilisation. Although owing to foreign invasions in the Indian subcontinent, the values of Hindu civilisation were battered and overlaid, yet never completely submerged, whether by Muslim invasions and Mughal rule, or the seaborne arrival of French and Portuguese adventurers, or the encroachments of the British Empire, complete with its implantation of representative political institutions and modern law. For India, South Asia is a strategic entity whose outer boundary forms India's own natural defence parameters. As a prominent power in South Asia, New Delhi sees the South Asian region as its sphere of influence. After India dismembered Pakistan in 1971, it began to see itself as the pre-eminent and pivotal power in South Asia. The Indira Doctrine, enunciated at the beginning of the Sri Lankan civil war in 1983, stated that India was entitled to be the security manager of the entire subcontinent. Another major factor, which has added to support this claim, is India's dynamic economy which comprises a diverse technological base that produces world-class software as well as rockets capable of launching satellites into space. To further its claim to being a great power, India is anxious to acquire a permanent seat on the UN Security Council.

Influence of Kautilya's Philosophy

Indian strategic culture is influenced by ancient Hindu political philosophers and one such is the thinker Kautilya. Even though the international environment has changed remarkably in certain areas, however, the teachings of Kautilya are still relevant to understanding India's strategic behaviour. The *Arthaśāstra* does provide guidelines to Indian leaders and strategic thinkers. India's negotiating style in various international forums and its position on various international issues bear a remarkable resemblance to the policies and positions which were shaped by the Kautilyan teachings. Kautilya's worldview was traditionalist—that the world is anarchic in nature; the objective of every state is to consolidate its own strength at the expense of other power. Be that as it may, it is a fact that the message of the *Arthaśāstra* remained part of oral tradition and fell out of the collective consciousness of India, till the providential discovery of its manuscript in the early part of the 20th century. A unique and purely Indian canonical text was available to describe the golden era of Indian history and the manner in which it came about.

Kautilya's *mandala* is ancient India's most notable contribution to political theory. Ensuring the state's security is based on the concept of *mandala* i.e. on the geopolitical assumption that there is a circle (*mandala*) of states, and a state's immediate neighbour is most likely an enemy (real or potential) and the state next to the immediate neighbour, by the *mandala* logic, is likely to be a friend. Indian strategic thinkers have adopted the central tenets of Kautilya's *mandala* in conducting foreign policy. India does not enjoy good relations with its neighbouring states and enmity with China and Pakistan is the prominent feature of its foreign policy. On the other hand, India has always tried to have good relations with Afghanistan, Iran and Russia since its independence.

To Kautilya, the only way of ensuring the security of the state in the *mandala* system is by the six-measure policy. Kautilya explained the measures as follows:

- **Peace**: Whoever is inferior to another shall make peace (with him).
- **War**: Whoever is superior in power shall make war.
- **Neutrality**: Whoever thinks 'No enemy can hurt me, or am I strong enough to destroy my enemy' shall observe neutrality.
- **March**: Whoever is possessed of necessary means shall march against his enemy.
- **Seeking alliance or shelter**: Whoever is devoid of necessary strength to defend himself shall seek the protection of another.
- **Double policy**: Whoever thinks that help is necessary to work out an end, shall make peace with one and wage war with the other.

A caveat is apparent in Kautilya's meaning of the phrase "conquering the world." He meant conquering up to what is regarded as the natural borders of India, from the Himalaya sin the north all the way south to the Indian Ocean, and from the Arabian Sea to the Bay of Bengal. Kautilya had said, "the region of the sovereign ruler extends northwards between the Himavat and the sea, one thousand *yojanas* in extent across." In the Indian tradition, the world conqueror, or *cakravartin,* was not one who conquered regions beyond the borders of India. In short, India did not include the land of "barbarians" or *mlecchas,* those outside of Indian culture.

Chanakya argued that power breeds more power but the challenge was to initiate the process with limited resources. His genius lay in offering insights for meeting the challenge of maintaining independence and becoming prosperous.

- First, according to Kautilya, economic prosperity strengthened national security and brought happiness to people, but it was not sustainable unless the gains were distributed fairly.
- Second, he emphasised the role of good institutions for internal stability. He considered rule of law (and not rule by law), essential for protection of private property rights and constraining the predatory or extortionary behaviour of rulers and bureaucrats. Internal stability, in turn, was essential for acquisition of knowledge and accumulation of capital.
- Third, he emphasised good governance, which meant having a clean, caring and competent administration so that resources were not siphoned off from building infrastructure to personal usage.
- Fourth, a judicious blend of moral and material incentives was necessary to elicit optimum effort from the king at the top to the herdsman at the bottom of the economic pyramid.
- Fifth, changes could be brought only through co-operation and coordination and not through confrontation and coercion.
- Sixth, it was a king's moral duty and in his self-interest to behave like a loyal servant to his royal people.

As a political realist, Kautilya assumed that every nation acts to maximise power and self-interest, and therefore moral principles or obligations have little or no force in actions among nations. While it is good to have an ally, the alliance will last only as long as it is in that ally's as well as one's own self-interest, because "an ally looks to the securing of his own interests in the event of simultaneity of calamities and in the event of the growth of the enemy's power." Whether one goes to war or remains at peace depends entirely upon the self-interest or advantage to one's kingdom: "War and peace are considered solely from the point of view of profit." One keeps an ally not because of good will or moral obligation, but because one is strong and can advance ones own self-interest as well as the self-interest of the ally, for "when one has an army, one's ally remains friendly, and even the enemy becomes friendly."

Because nations always act in their political, economic, and military self-interest, even times of peace have the potential to turn abruptly into times of war, allies into enemies, and even enemies into allies. It must be remembered that Kautilya was describing a foreign policy, not of a great empire like that of the Mauryas, but of small warring states in incessant conflict, such as India experienced before the Mauryan empire came into being. In Kautilya's mind, treaties were agreements between kingdoms of roughly equal power, agreements a king should break if they are no longer advantageous, and believing that a treaty will provide a wall of protection against a strong enemy would be a foolish act.

Kautilya assumed that peaceful empires cannot last forever, and that conflict among smaller states is more common in history. However, he did not believe that nations never act in an altruistic manner—indeed, Kautilya advocated humanitarian acts that also coincided with one's self-interest—but he did believe that one must assume, if entrusted with political or military power, that one's neighbours will eventually act in their own interests. Put another way, one would be betraying one's own people if one did not assume a worst-case scenario. A nation forced to rely on the kindness of neighbouring states is weak and, unless it can change rapidly, is doomed to destruction.

In his section on foreign policy, Kautilya wrote of the types of warfare as open war, concealed war and silent war. Open war is obvious, and concealed war is guerrilla warfare in modern parlance, but silent war was a differently articulated mode. It was warfare with another kingdom in which the king and his ministers—and unknowingly, the people—all act publicly as if they were at peace with the opposing kingdom, but all the while secret agents and spies are assassinating important leaders in the other kingdom, creating divisions among key ministers and classes, and spreading propaganda and disinformation. This concept of secret war was an original one and, in many ways, is a description of the cold war of the 20th century.

If one were to categorise or typecast Indian strategic culture, it would be evident that India was never theocratic. Hinduism is basically non-proselytising in nature. India also does it fit into the frontier expansionist category as Indians have never displayed any keenness to go beyond the Indian subcontinent, which is amply evident from history: there were few Indian travellers who visited other dynasties or civilisations. Imperialist culture, to a certain extent, existed during the Mughal era albeit within the subcontinent only. With India having missed the Industrial Revolution altogether, it obviously did not fit into the revolutionary technocratic kind of strategic culture either. India's strategic culture, therefore, stands apart from other strategic matrices.

Moralpolitik is the predominant feature of Indian strategic culture. It has been influenced by India's historical, religious and geographical realities. Thus, Indian history is an important source for understanding Indian strategic culture. In this context, it is important to consider how Indian strategic culture has been influenced by Kautilya's teachings. Kautilya did advocate the use of deceit to attain one's objective and such methods as wearing a mask of moral probity, religious righteousness or citing moral righteousness to mask one's intentions finds its justification and practice in Hindu religious texts. A study of the two epics, Ramayana and Mahabharata, provides a better understanding of the Indian propensity to take a high moral position publicly but to secretly and deviously act otherwise.

In a society dominated by religion, Kautilya's strategies for the consolidation of a monarch's power were dependent on non-religious factors. In a time period where a monarch's rule was believed to be divinely sanctioned, Kautilya held two levels of rule solidification and rule maintenance based on non-religious principles. He based his monarch's rule on the concept of *dharma* (right conduct, duty, law, social justice and responsibility). Although the concept of *dharma* has deep roots in Hinduism and Buddhism, the theory, quite secular in its content, was a practical and workable social ethic, and had little to do with religion or theology. The concept included social ideals such as tolerance and respect for others, even those with different religions and backgrounds, love of the family, compassion, which includes kindness toward slaves and prisoners. Owing to his adoption of the concept of *dharma* as quintessential to a monarch's rule, Kautilya moved away from the religiously-sanctioned rule by kings to one based on the concept of duty and social justice.

Good governance is basic to the Kautilyan idea of administration. Good governance and stability are inextricably linked. If rulers are responsive, accountable, removable, recallable, there is stability. If not, there is instability. Kautilya's precepts may have been in the context of the monarchical set up but they have all the more importance in a democracy.

A New Look at Diplomacy

Throughout history, many of the great names associated with warfare understood the far-reaching impacts of the military beyond pure violence and destruction. A study of the military theory and practice clearly reveals not only a capability by the military to operate beyond the realm of pure warfare, but also a need to apply its capabilities across the spectrum of national power. There is a close relationship of foreign policy and the power of the military. Military leaders must, therefore, conduct diplomatically-related activities in peacetime in order to fully understand and shape the environment prior to implementing any wartime action.

Diplomacy is an important substitute for military capacity. Military diplomacy is one of the tools in the conduct of a country's diplomacy. India has disregarded military diplomacy and the possible contribution the vast resource of trained and educated cadre available within the military, who can fill this crucial gap. Military measures during tense political situations must be part of a comprehensive diplomatic plan that includes negotiating benchmarks and clear escalation/de-escalation plans with concrete outcomes in mind. The plan and intended effects, including incentives or disincentives for intended response, must be communicated to the other party. Any political power must ensure that its protagonists are privy to its options and understood them correctly.

A strong Indian Armed Forces is vital to advancing international peace, stability and the human security agenda. As some of India's most visible ambassadors abroad, the Indian Armed Forces carry Indian values to the world and play a significant role in building peace—from deterring aggression, to delivering humanitarian aid, to the support that they provide to aid and volunteer groups on the ground. The inescapable reality is that India's strategic culture will not change of itself. The environment and threats will dictate the course it will follow. Defence diplomacy serves specific national foreign and security policy objectives. The military trajectory has great potential in the future course of Indian foreign policy.

Warfare in the information age has placed greater emphasis on influencing political and military leaders, as well as populations, to resolve conflict. A study of the great minds of military theory and practice clearly reveals not only a capability by the military to operate beyond the realm of pure warfare, but also a need to aptly apply these capabilities across the spectrum of national power. India can no longer afford to be oblivious about the balance of power across its national frontiers. Not only is it necessary to understand global politics and how it affects the country, it is necessary to shape the global balance of power in a manner consistent with national interests. The age-old grand strategy of keeping the country together must, therefore, shed its sub-continental preoccupation and also concern itself with maximising and projecting national power. Kautilya's *Arthashastra* teaches us this. If India does not enter a virtuous cycle of achieving success, prosperity and unity it risks falling into the vicious cycle of failure, penury and ultimately, disintegration.

Looking ahead, it is reasonable to assert that India's military diplomacy needs greater traction in the coming years. There will be greater regional and international demand for India's military services, support and cooperation. As its interests expand, India will have to secure them far from its shores and reach out and build defence partnerships with countries big and small. As India works to resolve the tensions between new national security imperatives and the inherited ideology of nonalignment, it should focus on the emerging relationship between military power and political purpose in India's global strategy.

Conclusion

The past is intelligible to us only in the light of the present; and we can fully understand the present only in the light of the past. To enable man to understand the society of the past and to increase his mastery over the society of the present is the dual function of history.

Throughout history, the rise of new powers usually has played out in zero-sum terms. Today, we face different challenges—from the financial crisis and growing income inequality to climate change, nuclear proliferation and international terrorism—that spill across borders and defy unilateral solutions. At the same time, political and technological changes are allowing huge numbers of people around the world to influence events as never before. And new players, from emerging economic powers to non-state actors such as corporations and cartels, are reshaping the international landscape. Thus, the geometry of power is becoming more distributed and diffuse, even as the challenges of the world are becoming more complex and cross-cutting. Even the building of coalitions for common action is becoming both more complicated and more crucial. Therefore, amidst all this change, as the world becomes ever more interconnected and interdependent, a just, open and sustainable international order is required to promote global peace and prosperity.

A zero-sum approach on strategic issues today will only lead to negative-sum results. The world needs to find areas to work together and strengthen diplomatic mechanisms that build trust and help manage differences. In a robust international order, India needs to strengthen and mature effective regional and global institutions that can mobilise common action and settle disputes peacefully; to build consensus around rules and norms that help manage relations between peoples, markets and nations; and to establish security arrangements that provide stability and build trust. India has a stake in the success of that system. And as its power and capacity grows, it will face increasing expectations to shoulder a share of common challenges abroad and from its own people to solve problems at home.

All of these strategies to address the rise of new powers and the demands of a shifting international landscape reflect a fundamental lesson about what it takes to lead and to solve problems in today's complex world. It is no longer enough to be strong. Great powers also have to be savvy and persuasive. The test of India's leadership going forward will be its ability to mobilise its people and other nations to work together to solve common problems and advance shared values and aspirations. To do that, it needs to expand its foreign policy toolbox, integrate every asset and partner, and fundamentally change the way to meet its goals through, what is now being called 'smart power'. National security today depends on decisions made not just in diplomatic negotiations and on the battlefield, but also in the financial markets and on factory floors.

SELECT QUOTES

* A wise king can make even the poor and miserable elements of his sovereignty happy and prosperous; but a wicked king will surely destroy the most prosperous and loyal elements of his kingdom.
* A king of unrighteous character and of vicious habits will, though he is an emperor, fall a prey either to the fury of his own subjects or to that of his enemies. But a wise king, trained in politics, will, though he possesses a small territory, conquer the whole earth with the help of the best-fitted elements of his sovereignty, and will never be defeated.
* Acquisition and security of property are dependent upon peace and industry.
* What is anticipated is human; and the attainment of a desired end as anticipated is due to policy.
* What produces unfavourable results is impolicy. This can be foreseen; but misfortune due to providence cannot be known.
* Throwing the circumference of the Circle of States beyond his friend's territory, and making the kings of those states as the spokes of that circle, the conqueror shall make himself as the nave of that circle.
* A reducible or a conquerable enemy will, when placed between a conqueror and the conqueror's friend, appear to be growing in strength.
* Of two powerful kings who are on amicable terms with each other, a king shall make alliance with one of them who likes him and whom he likes; this is the best way of making alliance.

* When a powerless king finds himself attacked by a powerful king, leading a Circle of States, he should submissively sue for peace on the condition of offering treasure, army, himself or his territory.

* Though actuated with feelings of true friendship, the conqueror has reason to fear his ally, though of equal power, when the latter attains success in his mission; having succeeded in his mission, an ally of equal power is likely to change his attitude even towards the conqueror of superior power.

* An ally of superior power should not be relied upon, for prosperity changes the mind. Even with little or no share in the spoils, an ally of superior power may go back, appearing contented; but some time afterwards, he may not fail to sit on the lap of the conqueror and carry off twice the amount of share due to him.

* When it is necessary to make peace with a king with whom no peace ought to be made, defensive measures should be taken against that point where he can show his power.

* When battle is fought in daylight and in some locality, it is termed an open battle; threatening in one direction, assault in another, destruction of an enemy captured while he was careless or in troubles; and bribing a portion of the army and destroying another portion, are forms of treacherous fight; and attempt to win over the chief officers of the enemy by intrigue, is the characteristic of silent battle.

* The king who is sued for peace and also the king who offers peace should both consider the motive with which the proposal of peace is made, and adopt that course of action which on consideration seems to be productive of good results.

* When the profit accruing to kings under an agreement, whether they be of equal, inferior, or superior power, is equal to all, that agreement is termed peace (*sandhi*); when unequal, it is termed defeat (*vikrama*). Such is the nature of peace and war.

* When the friends are equally rich in gold, they may yet differ in qualities such as readiness to comply with requests, mag-

nanimous and munificent help, and accessibility at any time and always.

* That friend who maintains friendship with disinterested motives and merely for the sake of friendship and by whom the relationship acquired of old is kept intact, is a long-standing friend.

* That friend who, either when attacked or when in trouble, makes friendship for the security of his own existence is temporary and submissive friend.

* That friend who contracts friendship with a single aim in view and who is helpful, immutable, and amicable is a friend never falling foul even in adversity.

* Whoever neglects a friend who is being hurt with or without reason and who seeks help with or without reason despises his own danger.

* When the assailable enemy is capable of retaliation and when the assailant's rear-enemy, capable of augmenting his army and other resources, has entrenched himself on one of the assailant's flanks, then the rear-enemy gains more advantages; for a rear enemy on one of the assailant's flanks will not only become a friend of the assailable enemy, but also attack the base of the assailant, whereas a rear-enemy behind the assailant can only harass the rear.

* Kings, capable of harassing the rear of an enemy and of obstructing his movements are three: the group of kings situated behind the enemy, and the group of kings on his flanks.

* He who is situated between a conqueror and his enemy is called an *antardhi* (one between two kings); when such a king is possessed of forts, wild tribes, and other kinds of help, he proves an impediment in the way of the strong.

* When, after having put down the enemy, and after having grown in power, a friend becomes unsubmissive, the conqueror should cause the friend to incur the displeasure of a neighbour and of the king who is next to the neighbour.

* The conqueror should never help his friend when the latter is more and more deteriorating; a ruler should so keep his friend that the latter neither deteriorates nor grows in power.

* When a friend is as accessible to the conqueror as to the latter's enemy, the conqueror should first separate that obstinate friend from the enemy, and then destroy him, and afterwards the enemy also.

* When a friend remains neutral, the conqueror should cause him to incur the displeasure of his immediate enemies; and when he is worried in his wars with them, the conqueror should oblige him with help.

* When, owing to his own weakness, a friend seeks protection both from the conqueror and the latter's enemy, the conqueror should help him with the army, so that he never turns his attention elsewhere.

* An unsubmissive standing army is better as it can be made submissive by conciliation and other strategic means; but it is not so easy to collect in time scattered troops as they are engaged in their individual avocations.

* Keeping a mountainous or river fortress with all its resources at his back in his own country he should fight or put up his camp.

* When a broken army, reckless of life, resumes its attack, its fury becomes irresistible; hence he should not harass a broken army (of the enemy).

* Enemies from enemies, subjects from subjects, subjects from enemies, and enemies from subjects should ever be guarded; and both from his subjects and enemies, a learned man should ever guard his own person.

* Whoever imposes severe punishment becomes repulsive to the people; while he who awards mild punishment becomes contemptible. But whoever imposes punishment as deserved becomes respectable. For punishment when awarded with due consideration, makes the people devoted to righteousness and

to works productive of wealth and enjoyment; while punishment, when ill-awarded under the influence of greed and anger or owing to ignorance, excites fury even among the hermits and the ascetics dwelling in the forests, not to speak of the householders.

* If a King is energetic, his subjects will be equally energetic. If he is reckless, they will not only be reckless likewise, but also eat into his works. Besides, a reckless King will easily fall into the hands of his enemies. Hence the King shall ever be wakeful.
* All urgent calls he shall hear at once, but never put off; for when postponed, they will prove too hard or impossible to accomplish.
* The secret task of a king is to strive for the welfare of his people incessantly. The administration of the kingdom is his religious duty. His greatest gift would be to treat all as equals.
* The happiness of the commoners is the happiness of the king. Their welfare is his welfare. A king should never think of his personal interest or welfare, but should try to find his joy in the joy of his subjects.
* It's just as difficult to detect an official's dishonesty as it is to discover how much water is drunk by the swimming fish.
* In the happiness of the people lies the ruler's happiness. Their welfare is his welfare. The ruler shall not consider what pleases and benefits him personally, but what is pleasing and beneficial to the people.
* Exercise of power and achievement of results should be properly matched by the ruler in order to win over the people.
* Miraculous results can be achieved by practicing the methods of subversion.
* There are six major approaches to foreign policy. The first is a policy of maintaining peace with another state which is based on a treaty detailing the terms and conditions. The second is the policy of hostility which be followed if one is stronger than

the enemy. The third approach is one of inaction: It is most suitable when states are of equal strength. The fourth is outright invasion but this policy is recommended for the very strong. For the very weak is prescribed the fifth approach, i.e., seeking shelter with another king and wait for better days, The sixth and the last approach recommends a policy of peace with one king/state while maintaining hostility towards another; such a dual policy is possible if help is available from another state to fight the enemy.

* Many rulers have been destroyed by being under the control of the group of six enemies (lust, anger, greed, infatuation, arrogance, envy). Those with character should not follow their path, but preserve righteousness and wealth.

* The people help the ruler, who is just in his actions, when attacked while in a serious calamity.

* The whole of this science is intended to create control over the senses. A ruler acting contrary to it and hence not having the senses under control immediately gets destroyed, even if he be the lord of the four ends of the earth.

* A ruler with contiguous territory is a rival. The ruler next to the adjoining is to be deemed a friend.

* A mad elephant, mounted by an intoxicated mahout tramples on everything that it comes across. Likewise is a ruler devoid of the light of learning, advised by an unwise minister.

* A ruler, disciplined by learning, will be interested in disciplining his subjects. He will enjoy the earth unopposed, devoted to the welfare of all beings

* One who does not keep one's word and one whose behaviour is contrary to that of the people becomes untrustworthy to one's own people and to others. Hence (a ruler) should adopt the same mode of life, same dress, same language, and same customs as those of the people.

* A ruler with loyal people accomplishes his task even with a little help because of their cooperation.

* A ruler with character can render even unendowed people happy. A characterless ruler destroys loyal and prosperous people.

* A ruler who administers justice on the basis of four principles: righteousness, evidence, history of the case and the prevalent law shall conquer the four corners of the earth.

* Power is the cause for the forging of treaties. Unheated metal does not join with metal.

* The force of (an army) which returns to fight, without any desire to live, is irresistible. Hence a broken army should, not be harassed.

* In daytime the crow kills the owl. At night the owl kills the crow. (The time of fight is important.)

* A dog on land drags a crocodile. A crocodile in water drags a dog. (The place of fight is important.)

* The policy of *vigraha* (hostility)is to be followed if the ruler were to see that, my country, consisting of martial people or fighting bands, or secure in the protection of a single entrance through a mountain fort, a forest fort or a river fort, will be able to repulse the enemy's attack; or, taking shelter in an impregnable fort on the border of my territory, I shall be able to ruin the enemy's undertakings; or, the enemy, with his energy sapped by the troubles caused by a calamity, has reached a time when his undertakings face ruin; or, when he is fighting elsewhere, I shall be able to carry off his country, he should secure advancement by resorting to war.

* An army not under control can be brought under control by conciliation and other means. Wealth is the key to raising successful armies and having a peaceful and just kingdom, and Kautilya's political science brings wealth.

* Before you start some work, always ask yourself three questions—Why am I doing it? What the results might be? And, Will I be successful? Only when you think deeply and find satisfactory answers to these questions, go ahead.

* The serpent, the king, the tiger, the stinging wasp, the small child, the dog owned by other people, and the fool: these seven ought not to be awakened from sleep.

* The arrow shot by the archer may or may not kill a single person. But stratagems devised by wise men can kill even babes in the womb.

* From the strength of the treasury the army is born.

* Men without wealth do not attain their objectives even after hundreds of trials.

* Only through wealth can material gains be acquired, as elephants (wild) can be captured only by elephants (tamed).

* A state with depleted resources, even if acquired, becomes only a liability.

* Whoever is inferior to another shall make peace with him; whoever is superior in power shall wage war.

* The army may go to the enemy, or murder the king himself, and bring about every kind of trouble. But finance is the chief means of observing virtuous acts and of enjoying desires.

* Wealth will slip away from that childish man who constantly consults the stars: the only guiding star of wealth is itself; what can the stars of the sky do? Man, without wealth, does not get it even after a hundred attempts. Just as elephants are needed to catch elephants, so does wealth capture more wealth.

* Strength is power; happiness is the objective of using power. Power and success are interrelated. Power is of three kinds; so is the success resulting from its use... a prosperous treasury and a strong army provide physical power."

* The power of good counsel is superior to sheer military strength. Intelligence and knowledge of the science of politics are the two eyes of a king. Using these, a king can, with a little effort, arrive at the best judgment on the means, [the four methods of conciliation, sowing dissension, etc.] as well as the various tricks, stratagems, clandestine practices and occult means to

overwhelm even kings who are mighty and energetic.

* A single assassin can achieve, with weapons, fire or poison, more than a fully mobilised army.

* The Mauryan soldier does not himself the Royal treasuries enrich nor does he the Royal granaries fill. He does not himself carry out trade and commerce nor produce scholars, litterateurs, artistes, artisans, sculptors, architects, craftsmen, doctors and administrators. He does not himself build roads and ramparts nor dig wells and reservoirs. He does not himself write poetry or plays nor delve in metaphysics, arts and sciences. He does not do any of this directly.

The soldier only and merely ensures that the tax, tribute and revenue collectors travel far and wide and return safely; that the farmer tills, harvests, stores and markets his produce unafraid of pillage; that the trader, merchant and financier function and travel across the length and breadth of the realm unmolested; that the savant, sculptor, painter, maestro and mentor create works of art, literature, philosophy and astrology in quietude; that the architect designs and builds his Vaastus without tension; that the tutor and the priest teach and preach in peace; that the *rishis* meditate in wordless silence; that the *vaidya* (doctor) cures and invents medical formulations undisturbed; that the mason, the bricklayer, the artisan, the weaver, the tailor, the potter, the carpenter and the smith work unhindered; that the mother and the wife go about their chores and bring up children in harmony and tranquillity; that the aged fade away gracefully and with dignity; cattle graze freely without being lifted or stolen.

He is thus the very basis and silent, barely visible cornerstone of our fame, culture, physical well being and prosperity i.e. the entire nation building activity. He does not perform any of these chores himself directly: he enables the rest of us to perform these without let or hindrance.

Our military sinews, on the other hand, lend credibility to our adherence to good *Dharma*, our goodwill, amiability and peaceful intentions towards all our neighbour nations as also those far away and beyond. These also serve as a powerful deterrent against military misadventure by any one of them.

If Pataliputra reposes each night in peaceful comfort, O King, it is so because it is secure in the belief that the distant borders of Magadha are inviolate and the interiors are safe and secure, thanks to the mighty Mauryan Army standing vigil with naked swords and eyes peeled for action, day and night, in weather fair and foul, all eight *praharas* (dawn-to-dusk-to-dawn), quite unmindful of personal discomfort and hardship, loss of life and limb, separation from the family, all through the year, year after year.

While the citizenry of the State endeavours to make the State prosper and flourish, the Mauryan soldier guarantees it continues to exist.

To this man, O *Rajadhiraja*, you owe a debt for that very guarantee which is a vital sine qua non to our nationhood. Please, therefore, see to it, *suo motu*, that you are constantly alive and sensitive to the soldier's legitimate dues in every form and respect, be they his needs or his wants, including his place in the social order, and ensure that he receives them in time or ahead of time, in full measure, for he is not likely to ask for them himself.

This is so because before getting so completely wrapped up in his onerous, harsh and exalted charge, the soldier has assumed with good reason that the State, in return for his services, has freed him from all responsibility of his own present and future welfare as also that of his family back home in the hinterland. He is thus very clear in his mind when deployed at a distant border outpost or when campaigning in faraway lands that he need only look out in front for the enemy of the State and concentrate only on his military onus, completely free of all temporal worries. This assumption is a holy sacrament and an unwritten covenant that exists between him and the State. And rightly so!

If ever things come to a sordid pass when, on a given day, the Mauryan soldier has to look back over his shoulder prompted by even a single worry about his and his family's material, physical and social well being, it should cause you and your Council the greatest concern and distress. I beseech you to take instant note and act with uncommon dispatch to address the soldier's anxiety. It is my bounden duty to assure you, My Lord that the day when the Mauryan soldier has to demand his dues or, worse, plead for them, will neither have arrived overnight nor in vain. It will also bode ill for Magadha.

For then, on that day, you, My Lord, will have lost all moral sanction to be King! It will also be the beginning of the end of the Mauryan Empire!!

* The various kinds of dangers are: that which is of external origin and of internal abetment; that which is of internal origin and of external abetment; that which is of external origin and of external abetment; and that which is of internal origin and of internal abetment. Of these four kinds of danger, internal danger should first be got rid of; for it has been already stated that internal troubles, like the fear from a lurking snake, are more serious than external troubles.

GLOSSARY

acharya	head of an organisation/ teacher
adhikarna	book
adhyaksas	superintendent
agninidhána	fire pots
agniyoga	inflammable powder
ahimsa	the philosophy of non-violence
aníkasandhi	intervening space
ákranda	rearward ally
ákrandására	ally of the rearward ally
Aalabda labharthah	acquisition
amatya	prime minister
anga-vibhae	divisions of army
agni-samyoga	explosives
angula	finger (a measure of a distance of about 1.78 centimetres)
anibhritasandhih	open peace
aníka	group
anusaram	second best
aparipanita	without a definite task
apasírnakriyá	restoration of peace
akritachikírshá	undefined peace
aratni	a measure of distance (about nine feet)
arvatobhadra	all auspicious
ardhachandrika	half-moon

ashtáníka	one of eight divisions
asahya	irresistible
asamhata	a detached arrangement of the army into small bodies
ásana	neutrality/ withdrawal from hostility
asuravijayan	conquest like a demon
atharvaveda	one of the four Vedas (or scriptures)
atavibalam	forest tribes
atisandhi	deception
atisandhatte	gaining more advantages
attalaka	bastion
audaka	water fort
ayurveda	ancient Hindu art of medicine
báhútsára	bodyguards
bala	force / army
bhed	dissension
bhiksuki	mendicant woman
bhoga	snake-like formation
bhrta	mercenaries
bráhmans	members of the priestly class
cakra	wheel
capa	bow
capakuksi	centre of the bow
chamúmukha	face of the army
chakravartin	paramount sovereign
chaturanga	four-fold
dána	gifts
danda	wooden rod/ punishment
dandaniti	laws
dandavyuha	rod-array
dasiputra	son of a maid-servant
davpa	external relations

dhanus	five times the length of the forearm
dhanvana	desert fort
dharma	duty
dharmavijaya	conquest for the sake of glory
dridhaka	firm/steady
durga	fort
duta	ambassador
dvaidhíbháva	making peace with one and waging war with another
dvisadbalam	captured soldiers
entardvipam	river-fort
ghashásya	face of the fish
godha	alligator
gomútrika	cow's urine
grahapatika	householder
gunas	measures/ qualities
himsrika	pirate ships
janapada	populated territory
kákapadi	crow's foot
kapatika-chatra	fraudulent disciple
karma	action (procedure)/fate
krama	procedure
kshatriyas	members of the warrior class
kshaya	loss of trained men
kritasleshana	peace with binding terms
kritavidúshana	breaking of peace
ksha	treasury
kuddala	spade
kuthari	axe
kulya	canal
kuta-yuddha	secret fighting
labdh parirakshana	preservation

lobhavijaya	conquest out of greed
madhyama	central
magadhah	court bards
makara	crocodile
mandala	a finely patterned ring of concentric circles
mantras	religious incantations
mantrasáddhya	negotiation
mantrasakti	intrigue
mantrayuddha	treacherous fight
mauhúrtika	astrologer
maula	hereditary army
mitra	ally/ friend
mleccha	outcast/barbarian
mor	peacock
mudgara	hammer
muhurta	span of time (there are 30 *muhurtas* in a 24-hour time span)
náyaka	leader
navadhyaksa	superintendent of ships
nigraha	confinement or death
niti	ethical principle(s)
nitisastra	the science of principles
pádagopa	servant
padika	commander
palana	maintenance of law and order
pana	coin (an annual salary of 60 panas could purchase grain, sufficient for four meals daily for one Arya male)
parapurabhiyanika	chariots for assaulting enemy strongholds
paripanita	a definite task
párshnigráha	rearward enemy
párshnigráhásárá	ally of the rearward enemy
parvata	hill fort

patti	infantry
pauranika	storytellers
phalgu	weak troops
phalgu-bala	riff-raff of the army
prabhavasakti	the power to influence
pradara	breaking the enemy's formation
prakara	parapet
prakrati	constituent
prása	twin-handled short sword
pratijápa	counter-intrigue
pratistha	hold
pratiyoddha	opposing soldier
puroyanam	vanguard of a marching army
rajguru	royal advisor
raksha	protection
rakshita vivardhini	distribution among the deserving
rasada	poisoner
ráshtramukhya	chief of a district
rathin/ rathika	charioteer
sadanga	six-limbed
sadgunya	six measures
sakatamedhi	pillars
sakti	power
sama	a measure of distance (about one foot)/ quiet
samsraya	alliance
samádhi	reconcilement
samcarah	wandering spies
samghate	compact body
samsthah	local spies
sandhi	peace/ agreement of peace
sangramika	battle chariots

sanjaya	victorious
sakata	wagon
saram	best
sarpasári	serpentine movement
sarvabhauma	paramount sovereign
sarvárthasiddhi	success
satha	obstinate temper
sarvatomukha	facing all directions
sáma	conciliation / fourteen finger-width
samgha	independent principality
sastra	weapon/instrument/machine
satri	classmate
sattra	ambush
senapati	commander-in-chief
setu-bandha	irrigational works
srení	category of soldiers (gild levies)
srenimukhya	officer-in-charge
sthána	keeping quiet
sthane	halt
sthúlakarna	big ear
slokas	stanzas or verses
súdras	members of low caste
súnyapála	officer in charge of waste lands
suprathistha	stronghold
surunga	tunnel
surdhbalam	soldiers of allies
sutah	soothsayer
svapadavadha	dogs
swamy	king
syena	hawk
tantra	internal administration
tantrayuktis	methods

tapasa	ascetic practising austerities
tiksna	firebrand
trtiyasaram	third in rank
turyakara	trumpet-blower
ubhayavetana	double-agent
udásína	neutral king
udasthita	recluse
udyánaka	park
upekshana	negligence
utsahasakti	personal energy and drive
vaidehaka	merchant
vajra	diamond/thunderbolt
vardhaki	carpenter
vaisyas	members of the working and trader class
vainayika	training chariots
vanadurga	forest fort
vapra	rampart of a fort
váripatantaka	crocodile-like formation
vigraha	war/offensive action
vijaya	victory
vijigisu	king in search of conquests
visálavijaya	huge victory
vyasana	calamity
yajna	ritual
yána	marching
yogakshema	welfare of the people
yojana	a measure of distance (about 8 kilometres)
yuga	cycle of five years

INDEX